AF624337

Anthropology of Complex Society

About the Author

Gaya Pandey (b. 1954) is a retired Professor, Department of Anthropology, Ranchi University, Ranchi. He has contributed nearly three and half dozen articles in Journals of national and international repute and edited books. He has participated in two and half dozen national and international seminars held in India and chaired a number of technical sessions. He has to his credit 26 books published in Hindi and English medium on different branches and papers of Anthropology.

Anthropology of Complex Society

Gaya Pandey

CONCEPT PUBLISHING COMPANY PVT. LTD.
NEW DELHI-110059

© Author

All rights reserved. No part of this work may be reproduced, stored, adapted, or transmitted in any form or by any means, electronic, mechanical, photocopying, micro-filming recording or otherwise, or translated in any language, without the prior written permission of the copyright owner and the publisher. The book is sold subject to the condition that it shall not, by way of trade or otherwise, be lent, resold, hired out, or otherwise circulated without the prior publisher's written consent in any form of binding or cover other than that in which it is published.

The views and opinions expressed in this book are author(s) own and the facts reported by him/her have been verified to the extent possible, and the publishers are not in anyway liable for the same.

ISBN-13: 978-93-5439-046-3 (HB)
ISBN-13: 978-93-5439-047-0 (PB)

First Published 2021

Published and Printed by

Since 1974

Concept Publishing Company Pvt. Ltd.
A/15-16, Commercial Block, Mohan Garden,
New Delhi-110059 (INDIA)
T: 91 11 41101460, 91 11 25351460, 91 11 25351794
E : publishing@conceptpub.com, *W*: www.conceptpub.com

Cataloging in Publication Data--Courtesy: D.K. Agencies (P) Ltd. <docinfo@dkagencies.com>

Pandey, Gaya, 1954- **author.**
Anthropology of complex society / Gaya Pandey.
pages cm
Includes bibliographical references and index.
ISBN 9789354390463 (HB)
ISBN 9789354390470 (PB)

1. Urban anthropology--India. 2. Urbanization--India. 3. City planning--India. 4. Sociology, Urban--India. I. Title.

LCC GN395.P36 2021 | DDC 307.760954 23

Dedicated to

With all regards, respect and reverence,
I dedicate this book to my Late Parents
Ram Pravesh Pandey and Ansuiya Devi
whose blessings still guide me for work.

Preface

Anthropology of Complex Society is one of the papers taught in undergraduate and postgraduate departments of Anthropology in different universities in India. But there is shortage of such book in which all aspects of anthropology of complex society have been described systematically under one cover. Keeping this in mind, attempt has been made to bring all aspects of Anthropology of Complex Society under one cover to help students and readers. The book has been written in simple English language. The book became successful with the help of teachers, students and well-wishers. Hence, it is my moral obligation to extend gratitude and thanks in their names individually and collectively.

I extend my sincere gratitude to all those teachers and scholars whose contributions on the subject anthropology of complex society benefited me much directly and indirectly to accomplish the task of writing this book.

I am thankful to research scholars and assistant professors of the Department of Anthropology, Ranchi University who encouraged me to write this book in English medium.

I acknowledge thanks to my family members, wife Smt. Indu Devi, daughters—Sudha, Suman, Sarita, Anu, Son—Shekhar, Garandsons—Kushagra and Harshita who took every care of me in post-retirement period.

I am thankful to Sri Ashok Kumar Mittal and his Team at Concept Publishing Company Pvt. Ltd., New Delhi for typing and printing the manuscript of the book with meticulous care.

Gyaneshwari
Booty More
Ranchi

Gaya Pandey

Contents

Introduction

Complex society is a society of societies. It has plurality of culture, society, economy, religion, political organisation, ethnicity and language. Complex society is found in urban and industrial setting. The concept of complex society is opposite to the concept of simple society. Simple society is characterized by singularity of culture, society, economy, religion, political organisation and language. Simple society is found among tribals and peasants.

The book deals with characteristics of simple society and complex society and approaches to the study of complex society in anthropology.

Folk-urban continuum has been described in detail. It highlights the process of acculturation by which members of folk society have transformed themselves into peasant society and peasant society has transformed itself into urban and industrial society. The culture of folk society, peasant society, urban and industrial society has also found significant place in the book.

Rural and peasant studies in Indian context has found significant place in the book. Attempts have been made to provide a review of village studies done in different states of India by different scholars.

Caste is an important social institution in Indian society. Therefore, studies on caste system in India have been reviewed to highlight the main features of caste in Indian society—rural and urban.

The study of urban and industrial society has been the main focus of the book.. Therefore, attempts have been made to deal with studies of different scholars on different urban and industrial cities in India with a view to review them systematically.

Attempts has been made to describe the origin and growth of cities in India in different periods.

Concept of urbanisation and its impact have been highlighted in the book to know types, causes and impact of urbanisation on Indian society.

The concept and impact of industrialization have been dealt with detailed description on revolution, definition, recent trends and impact of industrialisation.

Civilization is a complex form of culture. Therefore, attempts have been made to describe different anthropological approaches to the study of civilization.

Institutions of complex society such as family, kinship system, religion, administration and network have been dealt in detail to highlight main features of complex society.

Town planning is an important aspect of urbanization and industrialization. Therefore, attempt has been made to describe basic elements of town planning and problems related to town planning.

The book also covers about the origin and growth of urban anthropology and its main theme.

1
Complex Society
Concept and Approaches

The concept of complex society is opposite to the concept of simple society. According to evolutionist anthropologists, form of society in the beginning was simple. But later on complex form of society developed. Therefore, in order to know difference between simple society and complex society, it is necessary to describe, here, the characteristics of simple society and complex society one by one.

Social-cultural anthropologists study culture. But culture is a social heritage. We are not born with a culture. Rather, we acquire culture in society. That is why our culture depends upon the type of society. If we are member of a simple society, we acquire simple culture. But, if we are member of a complex society we acquire complex culture. Thus, on the basis of culture we can distinguish one society from other society. Rural society has some features of simple society and some features of complex society. It lies between simple society and complex urban society.

In anthropological literatures some synonymic terms have been used for simple society. For example native, naive, primitive, jungle-*vasi*, *Adivasi*, little community, barbarous, pre-literate society, pre-industrial society, stateless society, homogenous society and folk society.

In anthropological literature, a number of synonymic terms have been used for complex society. For example town society, city society and metropolitan society.

Characteristics of Simple Society

According to social culture anthropologists, the simple society has following characteristics :

Simple Culture

The simple society is characterised by simple culture. The members of this society have simple lifeways, rituals, beliefs, dietary habits and laws.

Simple Social Organisation

The social organisations of simple society such as family, lineage, clan, and marriage are very simple.

Small Size

The population size and density of population of simple society is low.

Kinship-based Society

Simple society is kinship based. Members are dependent on kins from birth to death. All problems are solved at kinship level.

We-Feeling

Members of simple society have we-feeling. They call own group members as we and other group members as they.

Face to Face Relation

Members of simple society have face to face relation. They know each other by face and name. They call each other by kinship terms.

Common Interest

Members of simple society have common interest in collective living and economic activities.

Simple Technology

The technology of simple society is very simple and can be used by any member of the society. Their use does not require training and expertise.

Simple Division of Labour

Members of simple society have simple division of labour based on age and sex for different activities in society.

Family as Unit of Production and Consumption

All members of a family take part in production and all members of family consume the produce. Thus, family in simple society is both unit of production as well as unit of consumption.

Subsistence-oriented Production

Members of simple society produce for subsistence not for market.

Lack of Wages

In simple society, members do not hire labourers. They make exchange of labour, if required. Otherwise, they produce by own family labour.

Barter Exchange

Members of simple society exchange their surplus produce by barter system either in local market or neighbouring villages.

Reciprocity

Members of simple society have reciprocal exchange of goods and services with friends and relatives.

Redistribution

Members of simple society have redistributive exchange with their village heads and priests.

Existence of Haat

Members of simple society have concept of *haat* which occurs once or twice in a week. Sellers and buyers know each other by name, face and village.

Less Production

Members of simple society produce very less amount of grains and other things. They do not have large scale production.

Existence of Magic

In simple society one finds the existence of magic in production and health behaviour.

Simple form of Religion

Simple society has simple form of religion characterised by animism, animatism and naturalism.

Oral Tradition

Members of simple society have oral tradition. They communicate orally.

Art for Entertainment

The arts of simple society—dance, songs and magic are for entertainment not for sale.

Sacred Centres and Performances

Members of simple society have sacred centres in their villages in the name of deities where rituals are performed on different occasions.

Sacred Specialist

Simple society has own specialist to perform rituals at sacred centres on different religious occasions.

Collective Festivals

Members of simple society celebrate their festivals collectively with the help of village and village head.

Medicine Man

Simple society has its own medicine man whose advice is taken to cure illness.

Informal Social Control

Simple society has informal means of social control. Members are controlled by village head, village priest and council of elders.

Emphasis on Morality

In simple society members attach great value to morality. They attach morality to religion. For immoral acts, criticism is made and social punishment is given.

Characteristics of Complex Society

A complex society is characterised by following features:

Complex Culture

The complex society has complex culture. It has plural cultural, ethnic, economic, political, religious and linguistic systems. Here, people of different ethnic, cultural, religious, political and linguistic backgrounds live together and follow their own lifeways. Thus, complex society has complex culture.

Complex Social Organisation

Unlike in simple society, the social organisation of complex society is not based on family, marriage, kinship, lineage and clan. Here, social organisation is formed on the basis of region, religion, language and occupation. These social organisations play political role too.

No Depending on Kin Groups

Members of complex society are not dependent on kin groups. Rather, they are dependent on occupational groups and friend groups.

Big Size

The complex society has big population size with high density of population.

Existence of Secondary Group

Unlike simple society, complex society is not characterised by the existence of primary group. Rather, it is characterised by the existence of secondary group. Members of complex society do not know each other by name, face and locality. They have impersonal relation.

Formal Relation

Members of complex society have formal relation. On the occasion of birth, marriage, death and festivals they are invited to participate. They pay a visit and exchange gifts after getting invitation.

Lack of Common Interest

Members of complex society do not have common interest because they do not have common occupation. Each member thinks about own occupation, not of others.

Complex Technology

The complex society has complex technology for production.

Experts are required to handle the complex technology. Persons with technological knowledge are known as expert. They handle the complex technology efficiently. For expertise they are paid more and more.

Non-agricultural Economy

The complex society has non-agricultural economy which is based on business, service and labour.

Complex Division of Labour

Members of complex society have complex division of labour. Their division of labour is not based on age and sex. Rather division of labour in complex society is based on expertise, efficiency, ability, qualification and technological knowledge. Thus, complex society has complex division of labour.

Family as Unit of Consumption not as Unit of Production

In complex society, all members of a family do not take part in production, but all family members consume together. Generally, father works or sometimes father mother both work, but they consume with their all children. Thus, unit of production is individual, but unit of consumption is family.

Value of Experts

In complex society experts are valuable persons. For different kinds of work, different experts are required. They are hired and paid according to their ability.

Heterogeneous Production

The complex society is characterised by heterogeneous production. Some are traders, some are contractors, some are doctors, some are engineers, some are administrators, some are teachers, some are technicians and some are service providers. Thus, the production of complex society is not homogenous. Rather, it is heterogeneous.

Market-oriented Production

In complex society production is done taking market value in mind. Thus, production of complex society is market-oriented.

Profit-oriented Production

In complex society production is not consumption-oriented. It is profit-oriented in complex society.

Complex Distribution

The distribution system of complex society is also complex. Here, an individual who takes part in production is paid according to his/her ability. From wages or salary he/she meets the demand of family members.

Payment of Wages

In complex society payment of wages is made for service rendered.

Need of Capital

In complex society, there is need of capital for production, without capital production is not possible. For this purpose people take loan from government and private banks.

Money Exchange

The complex society is characterised by money exchange. Here, everybody purchases commodities by paying money.

Market Theory

In complex society market theory is applicable. Here market is purely an economic institution. Price of commodities is determined by demand and supply.

Depending on Market

The complex society is fully dependent on market. Its members are dependent on market for their day-to-day needs.

Different Religious Symbols

Complex society has different religious symbols as temples, mosques, gurdwara and church. It is because people of different religions live in different colonies and practice their own religions.

Existence of Secularism

In complex society people of different religions live together and practice their rituals and festivals. But, they are guided by the spirit of secularism. They have regards for symbols and festivals of other religion.

Belief in Science

Members of complex society believe in science for production and cure of diseases.

Control of Former Institutions

In complex society, there are formal legal institutions to control members of society. For example Thana, Police, Court.

Central Authority

In complex society, there is central authority in the form of chief, king or government.

Economic Class

In complex society we have economic classes like rich and poor.

Great Tradition

The complex society has great tradition of literates, urban and religious people.

Formal Institution of Entertainment

The complex society has formal institutions for entertainment such as club, cinema hall, parks, sites, tourist spots, hotels and markets.

Art for Money

The art of complex society is for money. Singers, poets, musicians, writers, artists all are involved here in earning money from their arts.

Administrative System

The complex society has administrative system which provide drinking water, education, road, electricity, transport, tourism and communication facility.

Communal Groups

In complex society people of different communities live in different locality.

Slum Area

The complex society is characterised by big residential buildings as well as slum areas.

Weak Moral Value

In complex society moral value is not so strong as in case of simple society. In complex society people are involved in making money by illegal means and immoral acts. As a result theft, robbery, dacoity, rape, beggary, prostitution and human trafficking are common occurrence. The morality is not attached to religion.

Existence of Corruption

In complex society one finds corruption in Governmental and non-Governmental agencies.

Existence of Unionism

In complex society, one finds the existence of labour unions and other kinds of association to fight against exploitation.

Anthropological Approaches to Study of Complex Society

We can discuss anthropological approaches to the study of complex society under two broad headings:

- Approaches of British anthropologists
- Approaches of American anthropologists.

Approaches of British Anthropologists

British anthropologist E.B. Tylor in his book *Anthropology: An Introduction to Man and Civilization* (1881) had attempted to know the origin and progress of complex society on the basis of his evolutionary approach. He was an evolutionist anthropologist. According to him, society in the beginning was very simple. As mankind made progress, the complex form of society came into existence. The complex form of society appeared during the most evolved stage of civilization. In the stage of savagery, the form of society was in simple form. During the stage of barbarism, the form of society was a mixture of simple and complex forms. But, in the stage of civilization, the form of society became complex. On the basis of his evolutionary approach, he concluded that the society of mankind had progressed from simple to complex form.

According to Tylor, in the stage of civilization mankind became resident of towns. Coppersmiths, bronzesmiths, potters and traders came into existence as specialists. People involved in non-agricultural works and trade began to reside at a particular place together. This gave rise to population density. In order to control large population central authority came into existence. Urban administration and ruling class were developed. Town planning was made and several buildings and colonies were erected. The economy of town society was not based on agriculture. It was based on trade and market. In order to keep the record of trade and market, numerals and accountancy was developed. In this way, mankind became the resident of complex society during the stage of civilization. Tylor had attempted to show the emergence of complex society on the basis of historical facts and evolutionary approach.

Another British anthropologist, Graffton Smith in his book *Origin of Civilization* (1928) had attempted to show the origin and development of complex society on the basis of historical facts and diffusional approach. According to him, mankind of all places were not able to develop complex society. Rather mankind of a few places were creator of complex society and mankind of rest part of the world were imitators.

According to him, Egypt was the only place where complex society in the form of civilization emerged for the first time. From Egypt, traits of complex society diffused in other parts of the world. He has attempted to show the development of complex society on the basis of town planning, administration, government, priest, temple structure, trade and market. These traits developed for the first time in ancient Egypt. Therefore, ancient Egypt was creator of complex society and people of other places of the world were imitators of complex society.

He was of opinion that inhabitants of ancient Egypt made dam on river and gave rise to canal for irrigation and intensive agriculture. In order to make dam on river Nile, a large number of population was required. For this work thousands of people began to reside at a particular place. In order to control this population, central authority was developed and government was formed.

Writing and numerals were developed to keep the account. When the work of building canal by making dam was over, large scale agricultural production took place. This was taken as blessings of Gods. Temples were erected in their names. In order to look after temple priests came into existence. They were the chief adviser of the king. The large scale agricultural production led the emergence of coppersmiths, bronzesmiths, goldsmiths, potters, carpenters, and village priests as specialists to fulfil the needs of people. Towns were planned and developed to accommodate large scale population of different specialisations and traders. Government and administration were developed to provide civil amenities and protection to town dwellers. Thus, ancient Egypt gave birth to complex society. The structure of its complex society were adopted by the people of the world. In this way, complex societies were developed in all parts of the world. Smith was also of the view that origin and development of complex society can be understood through historical facts and connection.

Another British anthropologist and neo-evolutionist V. Gordon Childe attempted to show the emergence of complex society through universal revolution. He in his book *Social Evolution* (1951) has described universal major revolutions in the history of mankind. These universal revolutions were as follows:

- Agricultural Revolution
- Urban Revolution
- Industrial Revolution.

First of all agricultural revolution took place in the history of mankind during neolithic period. This revolution made mankind agricultural producers from hunters and food gatherers. Settled village life came into existence. Domestication of animals was started. Clothes were produced. Agricultural revolution led the building of canal for assured means of irrigation by making dam on river. Assured means of irrigation gave rise to large scale agricultural production and domestication of animals. For making dams large population was required at a particular place. To control the large population in making dam, central authority was developed. A number of specialists and classes of people were attached to this great work of canal formation. Labourers were paid wages. Different buildings were erected for ruler, administrators, specialists and labourers. Thus, water-based agricultural civilization occurred in river valley. This led the formation of agriculture-based complex society having carpenters, potters and priests as specialist.

The second universal revolution was urban revolution. Urban revolution occurred in the period between 7000 B.C. and 5000 B.C. in different river valleys such as Nile, Indus and others. This revolution was an extension of water based agricultural civilization. When a number of specialists such as potters, coppersmiths, bronzesmiths, goldsmiths, priests, rulers, administrators and traders began to reside together in river valley to fulfil different demands of agriculturists, towns were developed. The planning of town was made and different buildings for different classes were erected according to the plan having wide road and street. These towns became examples of complex society. The urban revolution got momentum during British colonial rule. British colonialists and imperialists made colonies, capital towns, district towns, hill stations, railway stations, college towns and university towns to cantonment towns and shipyards wherever they went and ruled. Thus, in the development of complex society British colonialists and imperialists had played significant role.

The third universal revolution in the history of mankind was industrial revolution. It began in 18th century in England and ended in 1990. This revolution led the emergence of industry-based complex society. During British rule industries of different kinds were established in different parts of the world. In our country, industrialization was taken as a model of development for the people by the government. Large scale industrial complexes were established. Thus, industry-based complex society developed.

The above mentioned all three types of revolutions had occurred at universal level. As a result, agriculture-based, urban-based and industrial-based complex societies emerged in different parts of the world.

Now-a-days, we are witnessing one more revolution, which is known as knowledge revolution, information technology revolution, communication revolution and American imperialism. Its origin is taken as around 1990. This revolution has integrated the people of all simple and complex societies to the global village society through science and information technology.

Approach of American Anthropologists

An American evolutionist anthropologist, L.H. Morgan had attempted to show the origin and development of complex society through his evolutionary approach. Like British evolutionist anthropologist E.B. Tylor, he was also of the opinion that complex society emerged during the stage of civilization. He had expressed this idea in his book *Ancient Society* (1877).

Another American anthropologist in his book *Folk Culture of Ucatam* (1941) had attempted to show the emergence of complex society through the process of acculturation. He had developed the concept of folk society and urban society as ideal types of society and polar opposite concept. According to him, no known society of the world correspond to folk or urban ideal type of society in totality. Rather they come near or in between the two ideal types of society—folk and urban. He has put peasant society in between folk and urban society. From the Ucatam province of America, he had selected representatives of four societies—folk, peasant, town and city. The village Tuski represented a folk society, the village Chankom represented a peasant society, Diztas represented a town society and Marida represented a city society. He found that the folk and urban societies were developed not in isolation. Rather they showed continuity, interaction and interdependence. Although folk society and urban society presented two different types of lifestyle, but they were not in isolation. They were interrelated. The transformation of folk society occurred into peasant society through acculturation. Again the transformation of peasant society into town society took place due to acculturation process. The town society developed into city society due to acculturation process. Thus, transformation of society from folk to urban was a continuous process and result of acculturation. Thus, the process of acculturation was responsible for the emergence of complex urban society from simple folk society.

Redfield tried to understand the emergence of complex society from the point of view of religious civilization. According to him folk and peasant society have little tradition characterized by rural, magical and unwritten or oral traditions. The tradition of urban society is great tradition characterized by literate, religious and written tradition. The great tradition developed in religious towns developed on the bank of rivers, confluence of rivers or river with sea and on the bank of great religious tank dug for the purpose of worship in temples. The tradition of religious urban centre binds people of a region and on many occasions people of all parts of nation. Thus, great tradition has regional and national value, but little tradition has local value. The great tradition is full of moral and religious values for people of folk and peasant society. Although, these two traditions—little tradition and great tradition—developed at two places in two different societies, but they are not in isolation. They are interrelated and interdependent. On many occasions they interact with each other having regional and national spirit. Redfield had expressed his view in his book *Thinking About Civilization* (1955).

Redfield with his close associate Milton Singer had written a research paper entitled, "Cultural Role of City" (1954). They attempted to know the origin and development of city through the process of urbanisation. They divided urbanisation process into two types which are as follows:

- Primary urbanisation
- Secondary urbanisation.

The primary urbanisation process gave birth to primary urban centres on the bank of rivers or confluence of rivers and confluence of rivers with sea. These primary urban centres were orthogenetic in origin. They were developed as religious administrative towns. They had patronage of great kings as rulers. The Panda Pujari used to connect these great traditional towns with regional and national people having little traditions. These primary towns were regarded as pilgrimage centres by folk and peasant people of a region or sometimes whole nation. These great traditional towns played significant role in development of regional and national feelings. These primary towns were examples of primary urban complex society.

Through the process of secondary urbanisation capital, district, commercial and industrial towns were developed. These towns were heterogenic in origin. Its character was secular. Members of such urban centres were governed by formal institutions and urban administration.

Another associate of Redfield Mckim Marriott made the

concept of little tradition and great tradition a dynamic concept. According to him, little tradition and great tradition are not in isolation. They are complementary concept and both are dynamic concept. He developed the concept of universalization and parochialisation to highlight the dynamism of great tradition and little tradition. Parochialization is a process by which traits of great traditions are added and accepted by the people having little tradition. Universalization is a process by which traits of little traditions are added and accepted in great tradition. Thus, through the process of parochialization traits of great traditions are localized and through the process of universalization traits of little traditions are universalized. In this way, little tradition and great tradition are dynamic concept.

2
Folk-Urban Continuum

Introduction

The concept of folk-urban continuum was developed by American anthropologist Robert Redfield in his book *Folk Culture of Ucatam* (1941). Redfield was interested in the study of change and continuity in different types of society such as folk, peasant, town and city. In order to understand the process of change and continuity in societies, he developed the concept of ideal types of society. He termed these ideal types of society as folk and urban. He developed the concept of folk and urban society as a polar opposite concept. He placed folk society at one end of a pole and urban society on another end of the pole. He was of the opinion that no known society correspond to these ideal types of society in totality. But they come near or fall in between the two societies—folk and urban. He placed peasant society in between folk and town society and town society in between peasant and city society. Identifying the four types of society, Redfield attempted to show the continuum between folk and urban society. He developed the concept of acculturation to understand change and continuity between folk and urban society. According to him, the folk society transformed itself into peasant society through the process of acculturation. The members of folk society adopted the lifeways of peasant society through acculturation process. Members of folk society transformed themselves into town society through acculturation and adopted the lifeways of town society. Again members of town society transformed themselves into city society by adopting lifeways of city society. He found that peasant society was more close to folk society and town society was more close to city society. Again peasant society had some traits of town society and town society had some traits of peasant society. Town society had some traits of city society and city society had some traits of town society. Understanding such continuity from folk, peasant, town and city society, he was convinced that to the formation of town and city was not in isolation. Rather they show continuity from folk to peasant, peasant to town and town to city society. Knowing this continuity he propounded the concept of folk-urban continuum. His folk-urban continuum was an interactive and interdependent concept.

Before dealing with the concept of folk urban continuum, it will be the fitness of the thing to present here cultural characteristics of folk society, peasant society and urban society one by one in detail.

Characteristics of Folk Society

Robert Redfield had developed the concept of folk society in his book *Topezlane* (1930). He made anthropological study of a village Topezlane situated in Mexico province of America in the year 1927-28. He developed the concept of folk society on the basis of his study. He found the characteristics of this village as representative of folk society. According to him, folk society is an ideal type of society which is polar opposite of ideal type of urban society. The concept of ideal society is a mental construct and no known society correspond to it *in toto*, but they are found nearby it.

According to Redfield, folk society can be identified on the basis of small size, isolation, illiteracy, homogeneity, group unity, face to face relation and traditional lifeways. People have we-feeling and call each other by kinship terms. The behaviour of people is natural and there is no artificiality in their behaviour. According to Redfield, the folk society has following cultural characteristics:

Isolation

Folk society exists in isolation. Physically, it is non-dynamic. It has its own boundary within which it exists.

Small Size

The population size of this society is small and the density of population is low.

We-Feeling

Members of folk society have we-feeling. They call themselves as we and others as they.

Non-formal Relation

Members of folk society have non-formal relation. They can go and talk to anybody at any time without any formality.

Face to Face Relation

Members of folk society have face to face relation. They know each other by name, face and relation.

Primary Group

Folk society has primary group. All members are closely related as primary group. The family fulfils all needs of its members. Family is centre of social, cultural, economic, religious, political and entertainment activities. Its members are not dependent on secondary group.

Simple Division of Labour

In folk society, there is simple division of labour. The division of labour is based on age and sex. But this division is not like watertight compartment. It is generally duty of women to cook food but males and children also do cooking whenever required.

Homogeneous Culture

The culture of folk society shows homogeneity. All members have similar house, similar household articles, dress, ornaments, foods, food habit, language, rituals, festivals and traditions.

Tradition Bound

Members of folk society are bound by tradition. They regard tradition as laws formulated by their ancestral spirits, gods and goddesses. They do not dare to break the tradition.

Simple Technology

The technology of folk society is very simple. Each family has agricultural and hunting implements. Implements are handled easily by all members. They do not require expertise.

Family Unit of Production and Consumption

In folk society, all family members participate in production and have equal share in consumption. Thus, family is unit of production as well as unit of consumption both.

Existence-oriented Economy

In folk society, production is for maintaining existence not for market.

No Wages

Members of folk society do not pay wages for production. They do production with the help of family members. Sometimes, they do reciprocal exchange of labour with neighbours and relatives.

Reciprocity

Members of folk society have reciprocal exchange of goods with friends and relatives on the occasion of birth, marriage, death, rituals and festivals. This is non-market and non-money exchange between relatives and friends who have equal status in the society.

Redistribution

Members of folk society have redistributive exchange with head or *Mukhia* of the society. Each family pays some gift to head and head returns them on other occasions.

Independence

The folk society is independent in production and consumption.

No Market Theory

Folk society does not have market theory. They have local *Haat* where they exchange their produce through barter exchange systems. The exchange is also for consumption.

No Formal Control

The folk society does not have formal means of control. Members are controlled by own groups and society head.

Existence of Magic

In folk society, there is prevalence of magic. They take help of magic to cure diseases, to get rainfall, to get good harvest and to harm enemies.

Moral Bound

Members of folk society are moral bound. They regard moral as part of their religion.

Religion Prevails over Secular

Members of folk society provide religious value to their house, cowshed, household articles, agricultural implements, fishing and hunting implements, land, cattle, forest, mountain, river, tree dress, ornaments and so on.

Lack of Formal Laws

Folk society does not have formal laws. They regard their traditions as law and moral binding.

Chief of Equals

Folk society has the concept of Chief but he is chief of equals.

Characteristics of Peasant Society

The term peasant is used for those families who own land, do agriculture with the help of own labour. They subsist on agriculture. They do domestication of animal for milk and help in agriculture. They have own land acreage, animals, agricultural implements and house. They are not landlords or industrialised farmers who do agriculture for more and more income. They maintain reciprocity and hospitality with friends and relatives. Previously barter exchange was prevalent among them. But now a days, money exchange has reached in peasant society.

Robert-Redfield has mentioned the following characteristics of peasant society in his book *Peasant Society and Culture* (1956):

Settled Life

Members of peasant society lead a settled life in a village. They have name and boundary of their village. They have own house.

Own Agricultural Land

Members of peasant society have own agricultural land. They do cultivation of grains, seeds and vegetables in their own land.

Own Agricultural Implements

Each peasant family has own agricultural implements.

Own Animal

Each peasant family has own oxen, cow, buffalo, goat, sheep, cock, hen etc. to supplement income.

Prevalence of Sacred over Secular

The peasant society offers worship to their house, land, cattle, agricultural implements, tree wealth, water resources, grains, vegetables and oilseeds.

Agricultural Festivals

Peasant society celebrates festivals related to agricultural processes such as ploughing, sowing seeds, transplanting, weeding, harvesting, thrashing, winnowing and bringing grains in house. They regard agricultural produce as grace of ancestors and Gods. They offer worship to ancestors and Gods on the occasion of each agricultural process.

Land as Mother

The peasant society regards land as mother. They have high religious value for their land because it nourishes them with foodgrains. Grains are regarded as children of motherland.

Use of Grains in Rituals and Worship

Peasant society uses grains—sunfried rice, pulse, oilseeds, vegetables, tree fruits to Gods, deities and ancestors on the occasion of each ritual, festival and worship.

Industrious Nature

Members of peasant society are industrious by nature. They do hard labour to get production. They work day and night without caring for their health

Concept of Good Life

Members of peasant society regard their life as very good. It is because they are independent and feed not only own family members, but also members of other societies. They regard visitors as *Atithi*, a guest. For this, they are rewarded by Gods.

Agriculture as Superior Occupation

Members of peasant society regard agriculture as a superior occupation because this occupation is independent. Peasants are not selfish. They feed themselves as well as visitors, beggars, disabled and poor.

High Thinking

Members of peasant society are known for high thinking. They are far away from theft, dacoity, loot, crime, rape, murder and corruption. They have strong moral binding.

Simple Living

The living of peasant society is very simple. They live in simple house, have simple household articles and furnitures, wear simple dress and ornament, and eat simple food.

Primary Group

Members of peasant society live in primary group. The family fulfils all needs of its members. Members are not dependent on secondary group for any needs.

Independence

Members of peasant society enjoy independence in house, land, cattle wealth, tree wealth, agricultural implements, production and consumption.

Informal Relation

Members of peasant society have informal relation. They do not need any formality to meet and talk to each other. Any member can meet with other member any time without prior information.

Homogenous Culture

Peasant society has homogenous culture. They have similar house, household utensils, furnitures, agricultural implements, food, food behaviour, language, dress, ornaments, beliefs, rituals, festivals and traditions.

Tradition-bound

Peasant society is tradition-bound. They have high regard for traditions. Moral and religious values are attached to tradition.

They do not dare to break the tradition. It is because traditions are laws formulated by ancestral Gods and Goddesses.

Simple Technology

Members of simple society do agriculture, fishing, gathering food materials, animal husbandry on the basis of simple technology. They do not need any expert to handle them. That is why all family members participate in production.

Family as Unit of Production and Consumption

In peasant society, each family is unit of production and consumption.

Concept of Capital

The peasant society has its own concept of capital. They treat land, plough, cattle wealth, agricultural implements, manures, fertilizers and seeds as capital for production.

Haat (Bazar)

The concept of *Haat* (bazar) is prevalent in peasant society. They visit local *haat* (bazar) which occurs once or twice in a week for day-to-day consumption needs such as salt, sugar, spices, oil, dresses and others.

Exchange for Consumption

Members of peasant society do exchange of agricultural produce in local *haat* (bazar). But exchange is not profit-oriented. It is consumption-oriented.

Simple Division of Labour

In peasant society, the division of labour is very simple. It is based on age and sex but not like watertight compartment.

Small Size

The peasant society has small population size and low density of population.

Face to Face Relation

Members of peasant society have face to face relation. They know each other by face, name and relation.

We-Feeling

Members of peasant society have we-feeling. They call their members as we and others as they.

Reciprocal Exchange of Labour

Generally, peasant society does agriculture by labour of own family, but on certain occasion reciprocal exchange of labour is found to complete the work.

Reciprocity

Members of peasant society maintain reciprocal relation with friends and relatives through goods produced by them.

Hospitality

Members of peasant society have high regards for guests. They provide good hospitality to guests whenever they pay a visit to their house.

Kinship-based Society

The peasant society is kinship-based. It is controlled by family head, clan head and lineage head.

Informal Control

There is no formal institution to control members of peasant society. Rather they are controlled by kin groups.

Social Position According to Birth

In peasant society, members get position according to birth and generation.

Production Mixed with Magic and Religion

In peasant society, production is mixed with magic and religion. They take help of magic and religion to get good yield from the field.

Indian Village as a Peasant Society

India is a country of villages. Here 70 per cent population lives in villages and carry out agricultural or allied work for their subsistence. In Indian village people do agriculture, sharecropping and contract farming. They have oxen, cows, buffaloes, hens, goats as livestock for assistance in agriculture economy. As a peasant society, Indian villages have following characteristics:

We-Feeling

Indian village has we-feeling and sense of togetherness. Its members call themselves as we and other villagers as they.

Concept of Village Land

Members of a village have concept of own village land. Each village has its own boundary and own acreage. The village land is distributed among families of the village.

Face to Face Relation

Members of a village have face to face relation. They know each other by face, name and relation.

Common Occupation

All families living in villages have common occupation as agriculture, animal husbandry and allied works.

Homogenous Culture

Each village shows homogeneity in culture. They have common house, household articles, agricultural implements, food, food habit, dress, ornaments, language, rituals, festivals and tradition.

Informal Relation

Each member of a village has informal relation with other members of the village. They can meet each other anytime without prior information.

Simple Life

Members of each Indian village lead simple life. They wear simple dress, eat simple food, meet easily, and follow simple lifestyle.

High Thinking

The people of each village not only lead a simple life, but their thinking is very high. They are not indulged in corruption, rape, bribery, adultery, theft, dacoity, and other immoral acts.

Agriculture as Superior Occupation

Members of each village regard agriculture as superior occupation. It is because they are attached to such an occupation which is free from corruption. They are not selfish. They feed themselves as well as guests, *sadhu*, *faqir*, beggars, poor and others who are in need of food.

Observance of Moral Values

In Indian villages, there is dominance of moral values. Moral value is attached to religious value. Members believe that for immoral acts they are punished physically, mentally, divinely and monetarily by Almighty God. Therefore, they attach great value to moral acts.

Good Life

Villagers consider their life very good. It is because they lead a clean and virtuous life. Although they always live in poverty but they consider their life very good. They are not selfish. They do not lead life for self. They lead life for others.

Independence

Villagers feel independence in matter of production and consumption.

Simple Division

In village society, there is simple division of labour based on age and sex to run family smoothly. But this division of labour is not like watertight compartment. On different special occasions, all members cooperate each other.

Simple Technology

Villagers have simple technology by which they do agriculture and domestication of animals.

Reciprocity

Villagers have reciprocal relation with kins and friends through agriculture produce on the occasion of marriage, birth, death, festivals and others.

Reciprocal Exchange of Labour

Villagers do reciprocal exchange of labour at the time of doing agriculture and erecting house for which payment is not made but food and feast is provided.

Family as Unit of Production and Consumption

In villages, each family has own land, plough, agricultural implements and cattle. All members take part in production and all members take part in consumption. Thus, family is unit of production and consumption in villages.

Prevalence of Sacred Over Secular

In villages, people offer worship to house, cattleshed, livestock, land, river, mountain, forest, agricultural implements and other things which play significant role in their life.

Agricultural Festival

Villagers celebrate agricultural festivals during agricultural processes like ploughing, sowing, transplanting, harvesting, thrashing, winnowing and storing new grains in house.

Use of Grains in Worship

Villagers offer sunfried rice, purse, vegetables, milk, curd, *ghee* and other *pakwans* from agricultural produce to their ancestors, Gods and Goddesses.

Informal Social Control

In villages social control is maintained informally. The family, lineage and clan control the behaviour of members.

From above account, we can say that Indian villages have maintained their identity as peasant society. But now-a-says heterogeneity, concept of profit, competition in production, money exchange and profit-oriented production have found place in villages. Individualism is also increasing day by day.

Characteristics of Urban Society

An urban society is a group of families of different castes, tribes, cultures, languages, religions and non-agricultural occupations and classes. All live together as an urban society. The lifestyle of urban community is quite different from peasant and rural community. Here we live in crowd, follow the rules of formality. Here people are not bound by common sentiment. Individualism prevails. Dividing forces are more active than organising forces.

Like village community, urban community also consists of a number of small groups. An individual tries to enter into big community from a small group. This is a continuous process. An urban community is divided into town, city and metropolitan society depending upon the size of population. An urban society has following characteristics.

Complex Life

In town and city, people lead a complex life. Here, an individual has to meet people with different ethnic background, culture, religion, region, language, community, class and occupation. He/she has to make adaptation with these diversities continuously. He has to leave his traditional life and adjust with modern life ways. Here, he/she becomes more logical and less religious. He/she has to adapt with complex lifestyle.

Competitive Life

In an urban society, people lead life in competition. Here an individual has to face competition in every sphere of life. This society is competition-oriented. Those who become victorious in competition move forward. But those who are runner lag far behind the victorious ones. Here people have to become competitive in service, post and occupations. People have to lead their life in competition.

Flexible Social Class

In village society one also finds the existence of classes such as peasant-labourer, artisan, priest and barber. All these classes have fixed position in the rural society. Their positions are not changing. Here basis of class is social. But in urban society basis of class is economic. Being economic bases, the class in urban society is flexible. Here, class changes according to income. For example, lower class, middle class and higher class. These classes are changing with change in income.

Cultural Heterogeneity

In urban society, there is no cultural homogeneity. Here, one finds cultural heterogeneity. Here people of different ethnicity, culture, language, region, religion and expertise come and settle together. Along with their body, they also bring their cultural beliefs and practices. This shows cultural heterogeneity in urban society.

Man-made Environment

In urban society one finds not natural environment. He/she finds man-made environment. For example, road, buildings, colonies, offices, schools, colleges, universities, stations, bus stands, malls, post office, bank, park, cinema hall, hotel, planetorium, clubs, markets, multi-storey buildings, zoo and others. They are not made by nature. Rather, they are made by man. Thus, in urban society, members live in artificial environment.

Non-agricultural Occupation

In urban society, people subsist on non-agricultural occupation. For example, service, administration, trade, business, entrepreneurship real-estate etc. These are non-agricultural occupation.

Social Mobility

In urban society one finds social mobility. In this society members are not bound to their traditional caste occupation. Any member of any caste can select any kind of education and job. Here, people are free to select education, jobs and occupation of their own choice. Thus, social mobility is found in urban society.

Lack of Face to Face Relation

In urban society members do not have face to face relation. They do not know each other by name and face. Here, an individual does not interact with all members. He/she interacts with selected members.

Secondary Group

In urban society, people are dependent on secondary group. Here, all needs of members are not fulfilled by family. Rather members of family are dependent on secondary groups who fulfil their needs.

Formal Relation and Interaction

In urban society relation and interaction are formal. Individuals meet formally by prior information. They use terms like sir, madam, thank you, sorry etc. Their relation is not based on sentiment. They have selfish relation. As soon as work is over, they break relation.

Control of Formal Institutions

In urban society, there is no control of kin groups. Here, social control is maintained through formal institutions like Thana, Police, Court.

Urban Administration

Urban society has urban administration like municipality, municipal corporation and mega municipal corporation. Through these urban administrations, civil amenities are provided to towns and city dwellers.

Individualism

In urban society there is existence of individualism. Here, an individual remains busy in his/her own work. He/she does not think and care for others. He/she leads his/her life in own ways. He/she attempts always to fulfil his/her own wills, not of others.

Nuclear Family

In urban society, there is existence of nuclear family which consists of parents and their unmarried children.

Non-kinship Relation

In urban society people live with non-relatives. Their neighbour are of different caste, tribe, religion and language. They are not their kin groups like lineage and clan. But, they maintain formal relation with their neighbours on festive and ceremonial occasions.

Lack of Morality

In urban society moral bondage is not so strong. People are attracted towards lust and passion. They want to lead joyful and materialistic life. Here, an individual can indulge himself or herself in immoral acts to get money. He/she wants to fulfil his/her needs by any immoral means. He/she can sell himself/herself, can indulge himself and herself in corruption, black marketing, bribery, human trafficking, robbery, beggary and prostitution. He/she gives up his/him morality and humanity to get money through illegal means.

Artificial Life

In urban society people lead artificial life. Their house, talk, feeling, living, dress, food and food habit become artificial. They live in multi-storey buildings, have windows, covered with thick *purdah,* have painted air conditioned room, use electric bulbs and fans, work in dark room with electric bulbs, have wall decorated drawing rooms, use cell phones for conversation, have digital communication, use hello, hi, thank you, sorry at the time of talk, wear branded dresses, call father as dad, mother as mom, eat food with spoon and spark, use hair dyes, visit club, restaurant, and work like machine. Thus, entire behaviour of members of urban society becomes artificial. They do not lead a real life. Rather they lead artificial life.

Work and Holidays Culture

In urban society people live in work and holiday culture. They are bound by hours of work and holidays. They have to reach at work place at a fixed time. They have to perform duty for a fixed hours such as 8 hours or 10 hours. When duty is over, they return home. They avail Sunday and national-state holidays. They have earned and casual leave facility. They visit market, park, tourist places or hotels during holidays.

Complex Marital Life

In urban society, one finds the existence of intercaste and inter-religious marriage. Husband and wife do not belong to same caste, religion, language and culture. They have to adjust with each other. Husband and wife both are working. Both are busy in own work and promotion. Both have different thinking of life. Such marital relation brings tension. There is no relative or caste members to release tension by making compromise. Husband and wife take help of divorce to release tension. After divorce, they arrange their remarriage with another partners.

Complex Technology

In urban society, there is complex technology for production. Production is made through machine and electricity. There are different experts to handle the machine and control the production. Thus, a number of workers are hired for the purpose of production. Things produced are sold in market. Money obtained from selling goods are distributed in the form of wages and salary to employees. The profit goes to the owners.

Market-oriented Economy

The economy of urban society is market-oriented. Here production is made keeping market value in mind. In the markets of urban society money market theory is applicable. The market functions on the basis of demand and supply theory. Here goods and services are exchanged through money.

Formal Means of Entertainment

Members of urban society have formal means of entertainment. For example, cinema hall, mall, Eyelex, club, hotel, restaurant, park, waterfall, tourist spot, zoo, planetorium, museum, markets etc. People can spend holidays and enjoy life there.

Corruption Culture

Members of urban society have to live in corruption culture. They have to pay bribe in different offices to get their legal work done. Administrators, clerk, officers all are involved in corruption.

Black Marketing Culture

In urban society people have to live in black marketing culture. People are dependent on markets for their various needs. But they have to face the problem of black marketing. Due to black marketing, they have to pay more prices.

Slum Culture

In urban society, the concept of slum culture has emerged. Slums are found nearby railway station, bus-stand, industrial areas, over-bridge, park etc. Here those people get shelter who do not have own houses. They come to perform different kind of work. In fact slums are dirty area of a town. Slum-dwellers do not get basic amenities. They are *thela*-pullers, rickshaw pullers, labourers and others.

Centre of Corruption

In urban society, a number of wealth related crime takes place. Poverty and unemployment facilitate corruption. On the other hand, the desire to become millionaire some individuals indulge themselves in crime, such criminals have protection of political parties and ministers and administrators. Taxes are levied, doctors, engineers, officers and traders are captured frequently. They are freed after paying a huge amount of money. Smuggling is a profession in urban society.

Centre of Sex Trade

In urban society, some houses or hotels are involved in sex trade. House owners or hotel owners have contact with call girls and their customers. They earn good amount of money through sex trade. Persons of good economic background are involved in such sex business.

Degradation of Religious Value

In urban society, there is degradation of religious values. Here, every work is done on the basis of profit and loss. People do not want to bear loss. Religious values and ideals are not taken into account. For them this earth is heaven and hell. One can avail the benefit of heaven on this earth by money. People do not follow traditions. They do not have time for prayer, worship, rituals, festivals etc. People accept scientific achievements gladly. They do not have faith in rebirth and life after death.

Time Money Culture

In urban society time symbolises money. Here, an individual utilises his/her each moment for earning money. Nobody wants to spend his time in vain. He/she utilizes his/her maximum time in earning money. According to urban people, time is money and money gives name, fame, status and prestige.

Mechanical Culture

In urban society, there is web of small and big factories. Mills, factories and industries are involved in production daily. As a result urban society obtained technical and mechanical culture. Here, an individual works day and night as a machine. His entire behaviour is shaped as per the duty hours in industries. He/she goes office by seeing watch, performs duty by seeing watch, have lunch by seeing watch, comes home by seeing watch, have dinner by seeing watch and sleeps by seeing watch and gets up by seeing watch.

Strike, Procession and Gherao Culture

In urban society, one finds the strike, procession and *gherao* culture. Different unions go on strike, lead procession, *gherao* and *bund*.

Culture of Selling Art

In urban society, the art is not for entertainment. Rather, it has become a thing of selling in the market. Here, musician, singer, player, poet, author, artist are engaged in selling their own art. Thus, culture of selling art has emerged in urban society.

Rearing and Caring Institution

In urban society some institutions have emerged which are involved in rearing and caring of children. For example *Aaya* culture, play school, nursing home etc.

Old Age Home Culture

In urban society, there is old age home culture. Here aged people live. Every care is taken for their health.

Folk-Urban Continuum

After discussing the characteristics of folk society, peasant society and urban society, the concept of folk-urban continuum is being discussed here. As discussed earlier that the concept of folk-urban continuum was developed by an American anthropologist in his book, *Folk Culture of Ucatam* (1940). Through this concept, he wanted to know answer of following questions:

- Can folk and urban society exist in isolation?
- Whether folk society and urban society interact?
- Whether folk society and urban society are complemented?

- Whether peasant society is a stage between folk and urban society?
- Whether peasantisation and urbanisation can be understood through the process of acculturation.

In order to solve these questions, Redfield propounded the concept of folk society and urban society as ideal types of society and polar opposite concept. Folk society and urban society as an ideal type society are polar opposite mental construct. It means that no society of the world will be similar to ideal type folk society or urban society. They will be nearby folk society or urban society or in between folk society and urban society.

In his book *Folk Culture of Ucatam*, Redfield made a comparison between four types of societies. They were as follows:

- Tuski—A folk society
- Chankom—A peasant society
- Diztas—A town society
- Marida—A city society.

These four types of communities representing the four different types of society belonged to Ucatam province of Mexico. He put Tuski as a representative of folk society on one end of a pole and Marida as a representative of city society on the other end of the pole. He placed Chankom—a representative of peasant society nearby Tuski and Diztas a town society nearby Marida. He attempted to understand continuity and change between folk society and urban society through the process of acculturation. The process of acculturation was responsible for transformation of folk society into urban society through peasant society and town society. First of all, the process of acculturation forced a folk society to transform itself into a peasant society. Then a peasant society transformed itself into a town society through acculturation. Finally, a town society transformed itself into a city society through acculturation process. Thus, the nature of society is changing. But this change does not put folk society and urban society in isolation. Rather, they are interrelated, interdependent and complement to each other. Although the characteristics of folk society are quite different from each other and polar opposite, but they were not in isolation. They were interactive and showing a continuous process of change through acculturation. Redfield found a number of similarities between folk society and peasant society. Similarly, he found some similarities between town society and city society. That is why he placed peasant society nearby folk society and town society nearby city society. When he made a comparison between peasant society and town society, he found a number of similarities between peasant society and town society. On the basis of comparison among four different societies, he came to the conclusion that no society exists in isolation. Though they accommodate changes through acculturation, but they maintain continuity in relationship. In this way, Redfield propounded the concept of folk-urban continuum. This concept can be understood better in following ways :

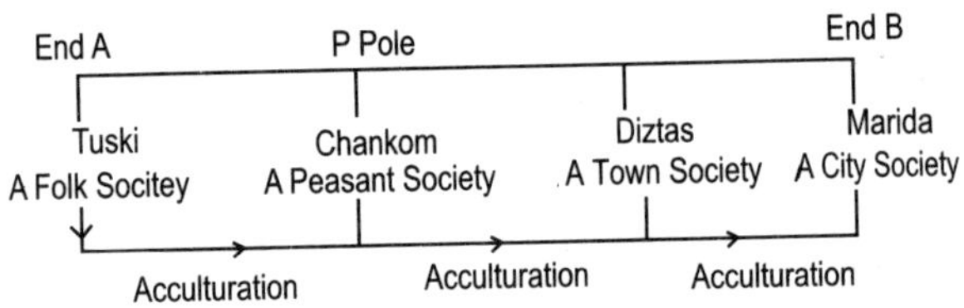

Folk-Urban Continuum

After establishing folk and urban continuum Redfield attempted to know the chief culture features of all four types of society. He found that a folk society is characterised mainly by moral value. The people of folk society places emphasis upon moral values. They treat moral values as order of Gods, Goddesses and ancestors. They do not want to lead a morally degraded life. They protect moral values and lead a good life. Contrary to moral value system of folk society, the urban society has technological system as its characteristics. Members of urban society do not pay special attention on moral value. Their entire behaviour revolves round technological system. Here, people are selfish. They lack human feeling. They establish or break relationship for selfishness. They have artificial relation.

According to Redfield, under folk-urban continuum a folk society comes in contact to urban society. Being in contact with urban society, some traits of urban society are included in folk society. As a result, some traits of urban society also appear in folk society. Now traits like isolation, homogeneity, we-feeling and influence of kin groups have become weak. Now traits like individualism, heterogeneity and secularisation have found significant place in folk society. Due to folk-urban continuum, the characteristics of folk society are disappearing. Importance of money has reached to them. Reciprocity and redistribution have become functionless. Now folk society has acculturated itself. The process of acculturation is true not only for folk society, it is true for any two societies which come into contact.

In his Ucatam study, Redfield presented isolation and homogeneity as independent variable and organisation, disorganization, secularization and individualization as dependent variable. According to him, as a society looses its isolation and homogeneity, it becomes secular and its members become individualistic.

Another American anthropologist Soltax had made a study of Guatemala society. He wanted to show that this society possessed small size and homogeneity, but family organisation is weak. Members have impersonal relation and secular value dominates. Here, members do not have we-feeling. They want to earn money by hook or crook. Reacting on Soltax's finding, Redfield said that there is no one reason for secular and individual behaviour.

Redfield also attempted to know the characteristics of peasant society. According to him, like folk society peasant society also possesses characteristics such as homogeneity, face to face relation, we-feeling, independence, strong family organisation, moral and religious value. But peasant society remains in contact with urban society for selling produce and other agriculture related items. The traders of town come to peasant to buy agricultural produce. Thus, peasant society remains in contact with town society. Due to contact with town society, peasant society is loosing its characteristics like homogeneity, we-feeling, religious and moral value and self-sufficiency. The family organisation has become weak. Secularism has found place. People have become dependent on towns and markets. Peasants visit daily to towns and cities for a number of needs. The village peasants have become indusrialized farmers. In this way, peasants have also adopted urban way of life.

Describing the characteristics of town, city and metropolis, Redfield described their characteristics as complete technology, heterogeneity secularism, individualism, and dependency on others. Towns, cities and metropolises differ from each other on the basis of density of population, but they possess all above mentioned characteristics. According to him, towns, cities and metropolises are centre of change. From here changing traits come in peasant and folk society and bring changes in their characteristics. Thus, he formulated such a methodology on the basis of which two societies found in two different ecological zones can be shown interacting and interdepending and incorporating changes.

The concept of folk-urban continuum propounded by Redfield has been criticised by Oscar Lewis and Soltax, both American anthropologists. Their criticism can be summarized as follows:

- Lack of definition of ideal type.
- Limited practical importance.
- Problem of empirical verification.

3
Village Studies in India

Village studies in India can be discussed under two broad headings:

- Village studies in pre-Independence period.
- Village studies in post-Independence period.

Village Studies in Pre-Independence Period

The credit of starting village study in India goes to a British evolutionist anthropologist Sir Henry James Summer Maine. He was a legal member of law in the Supreme Council of the Governor-General of India in 1862. He was also Vice Chancellor of Calcutta University. In his book *Ancient Law* (1861) he had discussed about the land system of Indian villages. With his keen interest in evolution of jurisprudence, he established in the book that land was held in common originally by groups of people. The book was based on his six lectures delivered at Oxford regarding usages and legal thoughts in the east in general and India in particular. In the second chapter of the book he had referred to the contribution of Pandits in the preservation of unwritten traditional law in India. He had attempted to show the common and collective ownership of property with a view to establish the theory of social evolution.

In his another book *Village Communities in East and West* (1871), Maine had discussed the characteristics of village communities in East and West. Under village communities in East, he had dealt with Indian villages having own traditions, land and collective living.

Earlier, a missionary Rev. William Tennants wrote a book *Indian Recreations* in two volumes (1803). In this book, there is a chapter on a village in Banaras district. Here, Jujmani system of the village having 100 population was presented.

A British administrative officer Baden Powel did valuable work on Indian villages and published two books *Indian Village Community* (1896) and *Origin and Growth of Village Studies in India* (1899). He had collected rich data from revenue settlement records, district manuals, survey records and Gazetteers. In the background of physical, ethnographic and historical conditions of the provinces, Baden Powel described the different types of villages. He suggested the idea of jointedness in place of collective ownership suggested by Maine. For Baden Powel, a village is a group of persons as well as an aggregate of landholdings.

An Indian Rev. Lal Behari Dey wrote a book *Bengal Peasant Life* (1874). In this book he had described the life of peasant community in a village Kanhanpura situated at a distance of 6 miles from the town Burdaman in West Bengal. The exploitation by *Jamindars*, British indigo planters and moneylenders have been described.

A. Aiyyar in his book *Economic Life of a Malabar Village* (1919) has described the landholding pattern and indebtedness prevalent in a Malabar village. Problems of wages and housing condition of workers have also been presented. Physical and mental health of villages and their festivals, education, unemployment, inequality and panchayat system have also been described.

Professor Gilbert Slater of Madras University did study of 12 villages and published his book *Some South Indian Villages* (1918). Data were gathered through application of schedule technique. The students of economics department were involved in data collection. The book deals with subsidiary industries, village trade, sanitation, education and village administration.

Dr. Lucas did study of a Punjab village and published a book *Economic Life of a Punjab Village* (1919). In this book, he has dealt with marriage rituals, education, sanitation, administration, political organisation, occupation, wages and indebtedness prevalent in a Punjabi village.

An economist H.H. Mann did study of two villages and published his book *Land and Labour in Deccan Village* (1921). Dr. Mann was Director of Agriculture in Mumbai. In this book, he has dealt with physical characteristics, landholdings, crop cultivation procedure, and agricultural stock of two Deccan villages. The actual economic condition of people as measured in terms of income, expenditure, and indebtedness have been shown statistically.

An another economist V.S. Ranade made study of a Konkan village of the then Bombay presidency and published his book *Social and Economic Survey of a Konkan Village* (1926). In this book, Ranade had dealt with social life, religion, daily routine and education of the village studied.

A famous linguist Sir George A. Grierson wrote a book *Bihar Peasant Life* (1926). He provided some basic informations related to a Bihar village. The vast area of the book covers inventories related to agriculture and household materials. It also highlights the real picture of a Bihar village.

J.S. Jack in his book *Economic Life of Bengal District* (1926) has described landownership, fishing and market facility in Faridpur district, now in Bangladesh. The role of debt and credit committee have also been presented in the book.

Radha Kamal Mukherjee in his book *Field and Farmers in Oudh* (1929) has dealt with landholding, livestock, agricultural processes, income, expenditure and loan among farmers of Oudh.

F.L. Brayne in his books *Village Uplift in India* (1927) and *Remaking of Village India* (1930) has described the impact of Gandhian thought in upliftment of an Indian village.

Strickland in his book *Rural Welfare in India* (1936) has described the impact of rural welfare in India.

In India, early social anthropological studies of village was introduced by a missionary W.H. Wiser. An American missionary Wiser was stationed in a village Karimpur near Lucknow in Uttar Pradesh. He did fieldwork at Karimpur and submitted his doctoral dissertation at Cornell University in 1930 under the title *Social Institution of a Hindu Village* (1933).

On the basis of his study he wrote a book, *Hindu Jajmani System* (1936). He with his wife Charlotte V. Wiser published another book *Behind the Mud Walls* (1930)

Methodologically, these books are based on intensive field-work in the village Karimpur consecutively for five years. Besides researches, husband and wife were involved in improving the conditions of low castes in general and Christians in particular. Since the village was under the direct influence of Brahmins, it furnishes an excellent model for long established Hindu village community. He had taken help of two Hindu youth as interpreters. Wiser had provided medical aids to villagers as a part of mission. Wiser—husband and wife with his two sons and two local interpreters worked for five years as a team and gathered data through particular observation technique.

The book *Behind the Mud Walls* (1930) presents the life ways of villagers. Leadership and agents of authority have also been described. The intercaste relation have found some description, but not systematically. No description about festivals has been given. The impact of caste system on the life of an individual has been presented. This book can be taken as an account of life in a North Indian village.

In his second book *The Hindu Jajmani System* (1936), the service relations of many castes with others where each in turn is master and servant, has been discussed. This system of interrelatedness in service within Hindu community was conceptualized for the first time as *Jajmani* system. Wiser describes Jajmani relationships prevalent among 24 different castes of the village Karimpur. Muslims and Christians were also involved in *Jajmani* relationship. He attempted to show changes occurring in *Jajmani* system due to education, manufactured goods, political movements, British administration and urban court.

The study of Wiser is of special significance because he had made intensive work in the village for five years. He had chosen *Jajmani* system for his inquiry. This is such a social and economic system which has provided employment in Indian society since centuries. His approach to relate all castes of the village including Muslims and Christians functionally and socially deserves special attention. He was of opinion that *Jajmani* system was based on ancient Hindu Law. *Bhangi,* Muslim and Christian were included as per local tradition in Hindu *Jajmani* system. In the analyses of Wiser the concept of purity and pollution does not figure at all. Later on, pollution and purity concept was introduced in *Jajmani* system. However, Wiser's study of *Jajmani* system is recognized as first detailed analysis of a complex exchange of goods and services among castes involved in *Jajmani* system. Thus, it was a first systematic village study in anthropological tradition. It is analytical and not merely ethnographic description of an Indian village.

After going through description of village studies in India in pre-Independence period, we can say that in this period village study in India was initiated by Henry Maine, a British evolutionist anthropologist. This was followed later on by missionaries, administrators, economists, geographers and anthropologists. The salient features of village studies during this period are as follows:

- All village studies were of general nature.
- In case of survey of specific villages only economic variables were taken into consideration.
- In some of social surveys, needs of social aspects were also realised.
- The need for empirical study was felt later on.
- In addition to socio-economic surveys, Wiser made an outstanding contribution by studying village intensively and in analytical manner.
- With the nationalist spirit for rural reconstruction in India under the guidance of Gandhiji, a number of economists and social reformers collected data about rural problems.

Village Study in Post-Independence Period

After Independence, village studies in India took a distinct turn. The call of Mahatma Gandhi to go back to villages was well received. The community developments were launched in villages. The Programme Evaluation Organisation was established by Planning Commission to undertake researches on villages. There were increasing contacts with American anthropologists who were interested in village studies. Scholars like Oscar Lewis, David Mandel Baum, Milton Singer, Morris Edward Opler and McKim Marriot did researches in Indian villages. Just after independence, Indian anthropologists M.N. Srinivas, S.C. Dube and D.N. Majumdar also took lead in village studies in India. As a result, a number of papers and books were published on village studies. A number of theoretical and methodological concepts were formulated and field tested and analysed to know the features of Indian villages.

We can discuss village study in post-Independence period under following headings:

- Village study in Punjab and Delhi Area.
- Village study in Eastern Uttar Pradesh.

- Village study in Western Uttar Pradesh.
- Village study in Assam.
- Village study in Jharkhand.
- Village study in Orissa.
- Village study in Bengal.
- Village study in Madhya Pradesh.
- Village study in Rajasthan.
- Village study in Gujarat.
- Village study in Maharashtra.
- Village study in Andhra Pradesh.
- Village study in Karnataka.
- Village study in Kerala and Tamil Nadu.

Village Study in Punjab-Delhi Area

In Punjab-Delhi area Oscar Lewis, a close associate of Robert Redfield of Chicago University America, did fieldwork in Rampur village and published two books:

- Group Dynamics of North Indian Village (1954).
- Life in a North Indian Village (1958).

Lewis had undertaken village studies in Mexico under the supervision of Robert Redfield. He had come to India as a consultant anthropologist for Ford Foundation. His field researches at Rampur continued for a period of 8 months from October 1952 to June 1952 with the assistance of seven Indian students. In this fieldwork traditional anthropological techniques like observation, interview, schedule, village census, life history and case study were employed.

In the first book *Group Dynamics of North Indian Village* (1954), he analyses the nature and function of factions prevalent in a Jat Village Rampur which had a population of 1059 at that time. This population was divided into 12 castes. The nature, number, size, age composition, economic and social characteristics and internal factors of factions have been described. The process of leadership formation and its practical importance for community development has been examined meaningfully. This work is of special significance because it was a first attempt to analyse factions of an Indian village systematically. The term faction has been used to denote groups held together by cooperative, social, economic and ceremonial relation. The inter-factional alliance has not been dealt.

The second book of Oscar Lewis, *Life in a North Indian Village* (1958) is a full length village study. The study brings out the total picture of the village Rampur. The villagers are presented as people rather than figures in statistical tables. The *Jajmani* system and factions have been analysed. The village festivals have also been analysed and described elaborately. Kinship, family and marriage have not found prominent place. The caste has been discussed in relation to Jajmani system. The caste hierarchy, inter-caste relations and rules of commensality have not been considered. He has proposed a functional definition of caste. According to him, a caste is endogamous social unit as the membership of which is determined by birth, it is often associated with a particular occupation and with restrictions about the acceptance of food and water from other caste groups. His analysis of small cohesive groups within caste called *Dhar* have been identified carefully and their functions have been analysed and well defined. These small cohesive groups within the village provide locus of power and decision-making process. These groups contribute to the compartmentalized and segmented nature of village social organisation. The book provides a comparative analysis of Rampur with Tepoztlan, a Mexican village studied by Robert Redfield. On the basis of comparison between Indian and Mexican peasant villages, illustrations about variety of cultural forms and need for a typology were done. Peasant villages of India and America were similar in material culture, level of technologies and economics and differences were in social organisation, value system and personality structure. In the light of such comparisons, Lewis concluded that the concept of peasant society was not sufficient for describing different cultural areas. He suggested that separate institutions developed at different historical circumstances and peasants showed inter-relationship with national culture and civilization.

The most significant conclusion on the basis of Rampur study was the concept of *Rural Cosmopolitanism*. According to Lewis, village Rampur is now not an independent village. Its members now have relationship with towns, cities, metropolises and even foreign countries. For work, study, health facility, business, trade and market. Thus, they are now member of cosmopolitan society.

In this way, he conceptualized rural cosmopolitanism to show regional, national and international relation of a village.

Dr. Indrapal Singh of Department of Anthropology, Delhi University, Delhi made a study of the village Deleke in Amritsar district of Punjab state. Under the initiation of Oscar Lewis, he worked in the village between July 1956 to November 1957 with grants-in-aid received from Robert Redfield of Chicago University. It was also a collaborative research with four research assistants. The result of this fieldwork was in two edited volumes, *Traditional India: Structure and Change* by Milton Singer (1958) and *Aspects of Religion in Indian Society* by L.P. Vidyarthi (1961).

In his first paper entitled, "A Sikh Village", Singh has given an ethnographic account of Sikh culture prevalent in a Sikh village. He has described as to how caste system and untouchability prevails in Sikh village. Villagers of different castes are broadly divided into two groups—(i) Sardars—upper castes, and (ii) *Mazhabis—Bhangis*. The two castes observe social distance. Both groups have wells and *Bhangis* were not allowed in Gurdwara till recently. The paper deals with Sikh culture written by a Sikh after a long training in village study. The paper does not deal with political and leadership pattern prevalent in a Sikh village. The inter-caste socio-economic relationship is also referred casually.

In his another paper entitled, "Religion in Deleke: A Sikh village", Singh has described beliefs and rituals practiced by villagers of Deleke. This village was located at a distance of 8 Km. from Golden Temple, Amritsar. The impact of Hinduism primitive supernaturalism and Islam has been presented on the Sikh village. The religion in Deleke presents a complete network of different faiths, beliefs and practices. Universalization of local Gods and Sanskritization of rituals have been referred. However, this paper remains to be more descriptive than analytical.

Village Study in Eastern Uttar Pradesh

The credit of starting village study in Eastern Uttar Pradesh goes to Morris Edward Opler of Cornell University, USA. Under the Cornell-India Research Project and under the Planning Commission, Government of India, Opler was attracted towards eastern Uttar Pradesh. Opler's continued efforts and repeated training programme in eastern Uttar Pradesh drew attention of a number of graduate students of Cornell University for village studies. Opler's collaboration with Lucknow University also provided incentive to a team of Indian scholars like D.N. Majumdar and S.C. Dube to undertake and encourage village studies in eastern Uttar Pradesh. Opler's effort of village studies in eastern Uttar Pradesh got success owing to his close collaboration with R.D. Singh, a resident of a village in eastern Uttar Pradesh.

Morris Edward Opler with his close Indian associate R.D. Singh made study of two villages of eastern Uttar Pradesh named Madhopur and Rampur in 1949. On the basis of study of these two villages, Opler and Singh published their two research papers. Their first paper was entitled, "Division of Labour in an Indian Village" (1948) and "Two Villages of Eastern Uttar Pradesh" (1962).

In their first paper, "Division of Labour in an Indian Village", Opler and Singh have described the intercaste relation and Jajmani system. In their second paper, a comparative picture of Madhopur and Rampur was presented. This paper was based on fieldwork in 1949 with the support of Cornell University, America. These two villages were of different sizes and different socio-religious environment. The village was located in a close proximity of Shrine city Allahabad. It had double population than Madhopur. The organisation of caste in both villages were also different. The village Madhopur had a population of 1852 persons distributed in 23 castes with Thakurs and Chamars as numerically dominant castes. 82 per cent land of village was owned by Thakurs. There were two Brahmin families also in the village but they were uninfluencing as they were dependent on other castes.

The village Rampur had a population of 3000 persons distributed in 24 caste groups along with 600 Muslims. Owing to the location of the village near the Shrine city on the bank of river Ganges, the Mallah (Boatmen) and Pandas (Brahmins) had numerical dominance. The Ahirs of the village were powerful due to their physical strength and aggressiveness. Thakurs were absent in the village.

In another research paper, "Economic, Political and Social Change" (1952), Opler and Singh had described the economic and political changes in Madhopur due to modern forces.

Opler in his paper "Extension of an Indian Village" (1956) had described the extension of the village named Senapur. In this paper, he had attempted to deal with network of the village

Senapur with larger units of Indian civilization. The network of the village Senapur with other villages, town, cities, metropolises and other centres of Indian civilization shows its extension. The villagers bring bride from outside village from the respective castes throughout the region. 15 per cent adult males are employed outside the village. Market towns, schools, colleges and universities, administrative centres, and religious shrines attract villagers. They influence them in many ways. Thus, the village Senapur has its local, regional and national extension.

The collaborator of Opler, R.D. Singh wrote a paper "Unity of an Indian Village" (1956) in which he had described the unity of the village Senapur. In this paper, Singh had attempted to answer two questions: (i) How can we identify an Indian village? And where should we look for its unity. He locates the unity of the village in oldest shrine that unites the villagers. Village Panchayat, the sentiments of villagers, intercaste relationships and other village institutions, play significant role in uniting villagers as inhabitants of one village.

One of the students of Opler Barnard Cohn published two research papers based on study of Madhopur village. Cohn had studied the cultural process for his doctoral dissertation on Chamar caste of Madhopur village. His second paper "Changing Status of Traditions of Low Castes" was published in Milton Singer's edited book, *Traditional India: Structure and Change* (1958). His first paper "Changing Status of a Depressed Caste" was published in McKim Marriot's edited book *Village India* (1955). In both papers, Cohn attempted to show the changing status of Chamar caste through cultural process.

An another students of Opler W.L. Rowe studied an another low caste of village Senapur for his doctoral dissertation in August 1955-July 1958. The title of his Ph.D. Thesis was "Social Mobility in Low Caste North Indian Community". It was submitted and awarded by Cornell University USA in 1960. Rowe had also written a research paper entitled, "Marriage Network and Structural Change in a North Indian Community" (1960). In this paper attempt was made to deal with exogamous nature of village community. As endogamous nature, villages have network relation with another villages. This also brought changes in social structure of the village. In his another paper Rowe described the contemporary functioning of *Jajmani* system in the village Senapur. He described exchange of services and economic activities of Noniya caste. He did not find any pressure and tension in *Jajmani* system.

Yogendra Singh studied six villages of eastern Uttar Pradesh. He was interested in knowing changing pattern of socio-economic relation in the countryside. He wrote a doctoral thesis on it and submitted to Lucknow University in 1960. In one of his papers, "Changing Power Structure in Village Community" (1961), he showed that upper castes and class continue to dominate in villages either direct and manifest form or indirect and latent form. The organisation was more in caste line than class line. Even at the caste level it took the form of faction alliances leading to increase tension and unrest in the village. The household continued to be the unit of participation as rural value system had not assimilated the secular democratic values.

An another scholar M.S. Luschinsky studied the village Senapur in 1954-1957 under the guidance of Opler and wrote an article on "Problem of Culture Change in Indian Village" (1953). In this paper, Luschinsky described the innovation in the field of public health, education, land reform and village government. The spread of innovation in village was determined by nature of message source, if human, its position in social hierarchy. The nucleus through which it was channelized in the village and its relative status in hierarchy and number of intergroup friendship ties and mediation nuclei.

In addition to Cornell University team, village study in Eastern Uttar Pradesh was also undertaken by D.N. Majumdar with students of Lucknow University. Under Cornell-Lucknow Village Study Project, he undertook microscopic study of villages. He also brought out his special number of journal *Eastern Anthropologist* entitled "Rural Profiles" (1955) embodying the findings of his team.

Along with several papers, Majumdar published a full-length book entitled *Caste and Communication in an Indian Village* (1958). This book was based on the study of a village Mohana under the auspices of Cornell-Lucknow Research Project financed by Ford Foundation. The fieldwork was started in 1953 and continued till 1955. Field investigators were employed for the purpose of study. The fieldwork was conducted with a purpose to analyse culture change induced specially by development programmes.

Majumdar had made a holistic study of the village Mohana in eastern Uttar Pradesh. The village had a population of 603 persons in March 1955 distributed in 15 caste groups. On the basis of intensive study, the short range history of village, inter-caste relationship, religious beliefs and practices, life cycle and other aspects of culture had been described carefully. Majumdar had considered village as a concept, as a way of life. For Majumdar, a village was a concept because it was a constellation of values which changed slowly so that village could retain its identity. The village was a way of life because people still lived more or less in the same way as they lived before. Majumdar considered village and town in India as two distinct constellations of value.

Majumdar had made an elaborative study of inter-caste relationship and processes of caste mobility. He described the process of fusion and fission which had produced innumerable social groups. He showed that caste mobility was horizontal and vertical with evidences. He was of the opinion that Indian villages were not a self-contained unity, it is integrated at different levels with total system of the country. He showed that each caste has a language. They use their own languages in communication with own members and also with members belonging to other castes.

The next book of Majumdar *Chorka Ek Gram* (1960) was based on study of a village Chittora in Mirzapur district of eastern Uttar Pradesh. The fieldwork was done in 1953 under Cornell-Lucknow Research Project under the direction of M.R. Goodall of Cornell University and D.N. Majumdar of Lucknow University. Chittora was a mixed village of tribals and Hindu castes. It had a population of 830 persons distributed in 12 castes and 5 tribal communities. Manjhi, Kherwar, Chero, Panikar and Bhuiya were tribal communities. The manuscript was originally written in English but translated into Hindi by Chandra Bhal Tripathy who was Deputy Director of Backward Class Commission. The book published only in Hindi presents a descriptive account of the village. It also describes the process of acculturation that were operating in the village. Although the book claimed to describe all aspects of village life but economic relationship between castes, festivals of tribals, political integration in leadership in village were not given adequate attention. The unity and extension of the village had also not been systematically described.

But in spite of these gaps, the book was of special significance because it dealt with such a village whose tribals and Hindu lived together. Tribals were detribalized and Hinduized. There were no dominant caste in the village. But this book was in Hindi and not available to English readers, specially scholars of Cornell University who sponsored this village.

Baljit Singh studied land reform in six villages of Uttar Pradesh with special reference to *Zamindari* system. He published his book *Next Step in Village India* (1961) in which he had described factions, casteism and social tensions prevalent in villages under study.

Another scholar R.S. Khare studied a village Gopalpur located at a distance of 33 km from Lucknow. Based on his study of Gopalpur village (1958-60), he published two research papers. His first paper, "Ritual Purity and Pollution in Relation to Democratic Sanitation" (1962) deals with relation between ritual concept of purity and pollution and physical status of cleanliness. He found that pollution occurs at the time of birth and death among relatives, but not physical uncleanliness occurred. Thus, he gave a new dimension to the concept of purity and pollution.

In his another article, "Folk Medicine in North Indian Village" (1963), Khare attempted to show that beliefs were determined by religious sophistication as well as social hierarchy. Folk medicine has an important function to release tension in the village. In practice of folk medicine hierarchy was not observed. All people were same before folk medicine man who practised folk medicine. Folk medicine is above traditional behaviour. This art was very simple and for all members of the village.

Village Study in Western Uttar Pradesh

In Western Uttar Pradesh, S.C. Dube under Lucknow-Cornell Research Project, made studies of villages with study team and published his book *India's Changing Villages: Human Factors in Community Development* (1958). With the help of four Research Assistants he made study of a Tyagi village and a Rajput village of Western Uttar Pradesh located in Rani-Khani block. Fieldwork was started in the end of 1954 and continued till 1956. The Rajput village had a population of 5142 persons distributed into 21 Hindu castes and seven caste-like groups of Muslim. The Tyagi village had population of only 757 persons. Dube attempted to explore cultural change in Indian villages through Community

Development Programme. The nature of study was evaluative. He had described human factors in community development.

An American anthropologist McKim Marriott of Chicago University, USA did rigorous fieldwork at a village Kishangarhi from March 1951 to 1952. His research expenditure was granted by Social Science Research Council of America. Kishangarhi was a Hindu village and had a population of 875 distributed into 24 castes, the most populous being Brahmins. The village Kishangarhi was located at a distance of 150 km south-east of Delhi in Aligarh district. This village was a laboratory for McKim Marriott for many types of researches. He had worked in the same village on caste ranking.

In the light of field materials, Marriott undertook to answer two types of questions raised by Robert Redfield of Chicago University. These two questions were:

- Can a village be conceived as a whole in itself?
- Can understanding of one village contribute to the understanding of culture and society at large?

Marriott had tried to refine the anthropological method of holistic analysis applied to villages of complex Indian civilization. Marriott wrote a paper, "Little Communities in an Indigenous Civilization" (1955). This paper was published in his edited book *Village India* (1955). In this paper Marriott tried to answer both questions raised by Robert Redfield. He propounded the concept of universalization and parochialization to answer both questions. Universalization is a process by which traits of little tradition are accepted into great tradition and through this process traits of little traditions are universalized. The parochialization, on the other hand, is a process by which traits of great tradition are accepted in little tradition. Through this process, traits of great tradition are parochialised or localised. In this way, concept of great tradition and little tradition propounded by Robert Redfield is a dynamic concept and does not exist in isolation. Both traditions are interdependent and interrelated. They maintain coexistence.

Dumont and Pocok in their paper, "Contribution to Indian Sociology" (1959) had criticized the concept of little tradition and great tradition. According to them, whether there was a little tradition in the same sense as there was a great tradition and the same relationship were held between them and between the corresponding communities.

Under the Cornell-India Project, John T. Hitchcock, studied a village Khalapur under the guidance of Morris Edward Opler. The village Khalapur was located in Saharanpur district of western Uttar Pradesh. Hitchcock was Station Director of Cornell-India Research Programme. He was stationed at Khalapur village. The fieldwork was carried out from October 1953 to July 1955 with the financial assistance of Ford Foundation and Board of Overseas Training and Research. Hitchcock was assisted by an interpreter who helped him in rapport establishment and data collection. On the basis of fieldwork in Khalapur village, he wrote a doctoral dissertation on the "Rajput of Khalapur: A study of Kinship, Social Stratification and Politics" (1956).

He had also written two research papers on the basis of his study on Khalapur village. His first paper was, "The idea of Martial Rajput" (1958) and second paper was "Leadership in a North Indian Village" (1960). In his first paper, he presented the ideal behaviour of Martial Rajput, which in actual process was weakened. The population of Rajput in Khalapur was 2000 who traced their descent from illustrious mighty king. They believed in their innate capacity as warriors and rulers. They also showed their descent from the king of *Ramayana* and *Mahabharata* to establish the martial character of Rajput. Although he had worked under the guidance of Opler, but he was influenced by Redfield and Milton Singer.

In the second paper on leadership, Hitchcock contrasted the two types of leaders prevalent in the village. One type of leader was traditional and other type of leader was modern. He considered village head and Panchayat as traditional leader and school Principal of intermediate college as modern leader. Both types of leaders were of same Rajput caste. Both type of leaders were drawing power from affiliation with outside agencies. He had also dealt with changes in leadership personality due to education, politics, urban influences and changing connection with wider system of nation and administration.

The same village Khalapur was studied by P.M. Mahar in the same period. She published her two papers. Her first paper was "Changing Religious Practices of an Untouchable Caste" (1958) and her second research paper was "Changing Caste Ideology in North Indian Village" (1960). In her first paper she had discussed the status of Scheduled Castes and their relationship with other castes of Khalapur village. She found that Rajputs of the village were occupying the dominant position in the village. But education, democratic setup, political parties, governmental institutions and administration had brought changes in the caste relation in Indian village. In her second paper, she presented the ranking of castes in Hindus and Muslims of the village Khalapur.

An another scholar John J. Gumperz studied the same village Khalapur in the same period and wrote several papers on socio-linguistics of the village Khalapur. He had identified social stratification in terms of linguistics differentiation. In his paper on "Dialect Difference and Social Stratification" (1958), he attempted to show social stratification on the basis of dialect difference. In his another paper, "Mass Communication and Media of Cultural Transmission", he described the cultural media through which cultural transmissions were going on. He threw light on social and religious network. He showed that elements of little traditions were accepted and included in the tradition of great communities and the elements of great traditions were accepted and included in little community.

An another scholar P.M. Kolenda worked in the same village Khalapur as a doctoral research fellow. On the basis of her field-work, she attempted to answer whether the people of India adopt themselves to the Hindu theory of *Karma* and rebirth. She collected data from untouchable caste sweepers. She established that great traditional religious ideas were not practised by sweepers, an untouchable caste. She observed a simple localised and parochialized form of religion. According to Hindu *Karma* theory, one's fate was direct result of one's conduct in previous life. Villagers were attempting to improve their status. Sweepers of Khalapur were interpreting the doctrine which suited in their own requirements for preventing and relieving misfortune in this world, rather than attaining salvation. Sweepers believed that fate and God were not absolute events and supernatural events existed independent of them.

Ralph H. Retztaff, another scholar associated with Cornell-India Village Study Project, studied the same village Khalapur in the same period and wrote his book *Village Government in India* (1962). In this book he had described the Village Government to analyse its functioning in historical perspective. A description of Village Panchayats had been furnished. He also examined the functioning of official village Panchayat which was started in 1949. Due to weak leadership of *Pradhan,* the official Panchayat had become weak and it was used only as a judicial body of Rajputs. Rajputs were the dominant caste of the Village Panchayat elections created always tensions and rivalries and reinforced the village factionalism.

Another American scholar Harold A. Gould studied in village Sherapur in Faizabad district in 1959-60 and 1960-62 as post-doctoral fellow of National Science Foundation and National Institute of Mental Health. On the basis of fieldwork, he had written several papers on *Jajmani* system, characteristics of peasantry and village exogamy. In his first paper, "Jajmani System of North India" (1959), he described the prevalence and functioning of *Jajmani* system in north Indian village Sherapur. The village Sherapur had 91 families distributed in 12 castes. All castes of village had service relation with washerman, carpenter and barber. Washerman, carpenter and barber were paid twice in a year in kind after harvesting *Kharif* and *Rabi* crops for services availed round the year. On festive and ceremonial occasion, they were paid food, food-grains, cash and clothes. The land owning castes dominated the landless castes. He was influenced by Wiser's work on *Jajmani* System (1936).

In his another paper, "Peasant Village: Centripetal and Centrifugal" (1959), Gould attempted to show the centripetal and centrifugal nature of Indian village. He found that village peasantries were self-contained and autonomous, but village was also dependent on urban centres and numerous processes of national culture. He called the self-contained characteristics and centripetal and dependent on urbon centres and numerous processes of national culture as centrifugal. He had identified three sets of experiences—

- Local reinforcing experiences.
- Tradition reinforcing experiences
- Modern reinforcing experiences.

He suggested that marriage represented the local reinforcing experience of the village and symbolised the relative power of centripetal tendencies in the peasant community. The pilgrimages represented traditional reinforcing tendencies, which symbolised the non-industrial civilization. Thus, Gould made a fascinating and refreshing analysis of interactional pattern in Sherapur. He found that Indian villages were centripetal and centrifugal both. He introduced the term Proletarianisation as a process by which low castes and classes had become defunctionalised in rural areas and were compelled to migrate to developing cities where they were absorbed as labourers in industrial complexes. In Sherapur upper castes and class were also becoming proletarianised because they were also going out to work in cities.

In his third paper, "Further, A Note on Village Exogamy in North India" (1961), Gould discussed the rule of village exogamy prevalent in Sherapur village. As it was a note, it gave us little about village life in India.

In his fourth paper, "*Jajmani* System of North India", Gould wrote about the structure, magnitude and meaning of *Jajmani* system in Sherapur. He presented systematically data on economic interaction. He attempted to examine three issues—(i) Involvement of relationship and payment in *Jajmani* system; (ii) Ecological unit for appropriate study of economic interaction in rural areas; and (iii) Relative magnitude of traditional economic interaction in India. According to Gould, the relevant unit of *Jajmani* relationship was a network of economic relationship whose spatial dimensions were not defined by corporate boundaries, but the location of households of specialists and their clients. He found that traditional economic interaction was prevailing in spite of economic and political upheavals. It was of fundamental importance for maintenance of social status and organisation. It was dependent on social organisation of Hinduism which was still strong.

Gould's model of *Jajmani* system integrated beliefs about pollution. But he ignored caste differences in capacity to pollute. But Kolenda showed difference with Gould. According to Kolenda, the roles of *Jajmani* and *Kamin* were not coordinated by fictive kinship as Gould spoke, but by a series of rules facilitating interaction of castes differing degree of defilement. She held view that it was quality of interpersonal relationship that integrated the system than rites and concessions themselves.

A.P. Barkabas studied a village of Saharanpur and published a book *Social Change in a North Indian Village* (1960). In this book he presented a comprehensive description of the village and identified the agency of change. He suggested a theory of social change also. He had dealt with family life, inter-caste relation, occupational pattern, political up-down, mobility, material culture, social control and socio-psychological change. He threw light on those factors which contributed to change and those factors which opposed the change. According to him, ability brought changes and institutional behaviour opposed changes. He had divided the book in three parts and sixteen chapters.

Village Study in Assam

Assam has been abode of tribals. Therefore, tribal study had attracted more attention than village study. An American scholar R. Burling made a study of a Garo village and published his paper, "An Incipient Caste Organisation in Garo Hill" (1960). In this study, he had described the caste organisation of Garo Hill village. One does not find any reference of a full-length monograph on village study. But few papers are available.

B. Bandhopadhyay in his paper, "Hira Potters of Assam" (1963) dealt with study of potters of two villages located in Goalpara district. He described the art of pottery making and pottery makers. The *Jajmani* relation of this caste was not described elaborately.

Saikia in his research paper, "Leadership Study in a few Assam Villages" (1964) had described the importance of traditional leadership and value of new leadership in context of six Assam villages. Attempts were made to deal with leadership of community development. The fieldwork was undertaken in six villages—Two in Tripura with 360 population, two tribal villages in Assam having 88 and 175 population, two non-tribal villages in Assam with 600 population. The research was conducted by Agro-Economic Research Centre for North-East India at Jorhat. The author compared the pattern of leadership in tribal and non-tribal villages and brought out differences between two types of villages. He found that traditional leaders were still powerful in tribal villages but in non-tribal villages they were not so powerful. However, some exceptions were there. Except in mixed villages caste-based leadership was absent.

B.M. Das in his research paper, "Kaharpara: A Report on Socio-Cultural Survey" (1964) had described the socio-cultural scenarios of Kharpara village. This was a unicaste village having 245 population distributed in 43 families. The village was located in Ravi block of Kamrup district; 9 km south-west of Guwahati. Its purpose was to know the socio-cultural life of the village. Villagers were dependent upon agriculture. The village council used to settle the dispute related to breach of social laws and customs. Only few aspects of village life were discussed. Kinship and initiation ceremonies were not touched.

Village Studies in Bihar and Jharkhand

The village studies in the then Bihar and present Jharkhand was confined mainly to tribal areas of Jharkhand. Vidyarthi studied a tribal village Ghaghara and published a book *Ghaghara: A Tribal Village* (1966). In this book he had shown that Manjhi; a section of Munda tribe used to call themselves as caste in place of tribe. They were influenced by Hinduism and celebrated Hindu festivals and worship.

Sachchidananda studied a tribal village and published this book *Tribal Village in Bihar: Unity and Extension* (1968). According to him tribal village also showed unity and extension like a caste village. Tribal village was also self-contained and independent, but it was also related to larger urban society and national culture.

N.K. Shukla in his paper, "Social Structure of a Bihar Village" (1968) studied a Bihar village near Bhagalpur and described its social structure. In this study, he tested a number of concepts like dominant caste, Sanskritisation and factionalism.

Village Study in Odisha

In Orissa, non-tribal villages were studied by F.G. Bailey, a noted British social anthropologist. Bailey carried out fieldwork at Bisipara village located at a distance of 12 km from administrative centre of Koldman of Fulbani district. The village surrounded by dense forest included 180 families with 700 population. Fieldwork was done under the guidance of H.M. Glackman in 1952-1954. Preliminary results were published in the form of research papers. The papers were first published in *Economic and Political Weekly* and later in Srinivas' edited book *India's Village* (1955).

The full-length monograph on Bispara was published under the title *Caste and Economic Frontiers* (1957). This book aimed at analysing the changes that had occurred in internal organisation of an Oriyan village Bisipara due to extension of its economic and administrative frontiers. It was a study of change in peasant economy which had occurred due to far long contact with traders, frontiers which was caused by caste system; government policies and other external contacts. Although Bailey was concerned with synchronic appraisal of the situation, changes in internal organisation were also reviewed diachronically since mid-19th century. Bailey examined the political implications of these developments in village. He pointed out the modifications in traditional political structure resulting from contact between simple peasant economy with modern world. Taken on the whole, the study was an excellent cross-section of the interrelationship of economic, social and political forces in Indian village. This study confirmed that in studying the microcosm anthropologists also studied the macrocosm. The study provided a historical perspective of an Indian village. The author examined the economic and political implication of Sanskritisation in the context of village as well as wider economy of the state.

Bailey's another book *Tribe, Caste and Nation* (1960) dealt with political changes in Highland Orissa. In this book he made a comparative study of the village Bisipara with the village Bederi. The village Bederi was studied in 1955. Taking materials from two villages, the study explored the political organisation of tribals interacting with political system of non-tribal counterparts of the region. The analysis was presented to show social organisation of tribes in relation to region and nation. On the basis of study, he pointed out that there were no accepted criteria for distinguishing a tribe from caste. A continuum between the two was more in reality. He suggested two ways by which a tribe might become a caste. But in modern caste which was active politically, both the tribe and traditional caste were being merged. Thus, attempt was made to show the adaptation of tribal system with caste system and finally with nation. It this way, modern political system had played significant role in Tribe-Caste-Nation Continuum.

Bailey published his third book, *Politics and Social Change: Orissa* (1959). This study is based on materials collected from the village Mohanpur which was in close contact with urban centre Cuttak than the other two villages Bisipara and Bederi studied earlier by Bailey.

This village had a population of 1300 persons divided into 20 castes. The village was exposed to external influence and locus of power resided outside the village. But the village had unity of its own with traditional village council, school, common village festivals and common observance of rituals and ceremonies.

Bailey distinguished three levels of political institutions in Orissa—The state, constituency and village. He attempted to examine their relationships. He tried to show social change in Orissan villages through three levels of political institutions.

The Department of Anthropology in Orissa was started in 1960. But no attempt was made for village study. But some local scholars had attempted to do fieldwork in Orissan village. Nityanand Patnaik did some problem-oriented village studies and published few papers on functioning of caste system in an Orissan village. In his first paper "Caste and Occupation in Rural Orissa" (1954), Patnaik had attempted to describe the functioning of caste Panchayat and caste occupation of Teli caste of an Orissan village located nearby the Puri town. He showed that Teli caste of neighbouring villages had its own caste Panchayat to solve caste problems. But they had occupational relations of the village. Thus, Teli were functionally related to other castes. In his second paper, "Outcasting among Oilman for Drinking Wine" (1960), Patnaik explored the practice of outcasting among Teli caste for drinking wine. He found the organisation of caste Panchayat very strong in oilman. It had power to outcaste a person for drinking wine. It was because drinking wine was not taken as good by Teli caste. If a person was found guilty of drinking wine, he was outcasted by caste Panchayat. But after seeking pardon and making promise of not taking wine, they are reabsorbed in Teli caste. In this way, regional Panchayat of Teli caste was very strong.

In his third paper, "Barbers and Their Clients in an Orissan Village" (1960), Patnaik described the status, roles and services performed by barbers in village Dumaria. The village Dumaria was located at a distance of 5 km from Rampur in Puri district. It had a population of 300 persons divided into 61 families and four castes. He found that barbers of Dumaria were performing services related to barber in the same village as well as neighbouring villages. Due to urban contact, some families had migrated to urban centres to work in saloon. They were not performing services to villagers. Barbers performing services in villages were paid in kind twice in a year and foodgrains, clothes and money on festive and ceremonial occasions.

In his fourth paper, "Assembly of Barbers in Dumaria Village" (1964), Patnaik had described the assembly of barber caste held in village Dumaria from 5th to 7th May, 1961. This assembly had a jurisdiction over 50 villages of the region. Thus, roles and organisation of barber caste was explored and described in the context of Dumaria village. Through this regional level organisation barber caste solved their problems and prepared themselves to face new challenges.

Village Study in Bengal

The tradition of village study in Bengal had a long history. Here Lal Behari Dey had studied a village Kanchhanpur in 1874. This village was restudied in 1933 and 1958-59. The study of this village was published as *Bengal Peasant Life Time to Time*. The book described caste economy, religion and family life prevalent in the village. Community activities, account of government sponsored Panchayat, indigenous welfare institutions, impact of land reforms, community development officers, and modern political movements were dealt with in detail. Changes had occurred at ritual structure in the village. The caste system was presented not in hierarchical vertical order. Caste system was presented by a concentric circle. Brahmins occupied central position. Four rings represented as follows:

- High castes.
- Jal-chal castes whose water was accepted by Brahmins.
- Jal-achal castes whose water was not accepted by Brahmins.
- Exterior castes—Santhals and Muslims.

Jyotirmoyee Sharma studied four villages of Burdwan district under the auspices of Burdwan Village Study Scheme organised by Henry C. Chart of University of Wilson in 1953-54. Data collected from four villages were analysed and presented in a long paper by Sharma, "Secular Status of Castes" (1955). He identified two types of status in villages—religious and secular. Religious status is based on tradition. Festive and ritualistic inter caste relationship among castes was maintained and controlled by it. Secular status is based on modern way of living and modern occupation. Modern inter-caste relationship is maintained and controlled by it. Thus, he presented caste hierarchy in modern context.

Working on the same material drawn from four villages of Burdwan, Lalit Sen published his paper "Families in Four Indian Villages" (1965). In this paper Sen traced the correlation of family type with caste, education, income, outside contacts and ownership of productive assets in Bengal villages. He found the dominance of joint family and extended family in villages, contrary to nuclear family in urban centres. The study indicated that in villages nuclear family was more in number among labourers and non-agriculturists.

Gouranga Chattopadhyay made a study of village Ranjana and published a full-length monograph *Ranjana* (1964). The data were collected between November 1956 and January 1960 with financial assistance of Ministry of Education. The author worked under the guidance of his father Late K.P. Chattopadhyay. The purpose of study was to find out the solidarity of rural values in contact with urban centres. He clearly brought out that rural values and ideas were changing due to contact with urban centres. He found that kinship bondage was still strong in villages. Processes like Sanskritization and Westernization were influencing the lifeways of villagers. The Santhal had adopted two local Hindu festivals. But the interaction between little tradition of villages with great traditions of towns and cities did not find any attention. *Jajmani* system also did find any place in the study. However, the book provides full-length anthropological picture of a Bengal village.

P.K. Bhowmik made study of a village Daharpur in Midnapur district. This heterogeneous village was located at a distance of 18 km south of Kharagpur in Midnapur district. The village had a population of 248 persons divided into 46 families and 10 castes. The Munda were at outskirt of the village. Based on this study he published a paper, "Caste and Service in Bengal Village" (1963). He described the prevalence of caste interaction in Bengal village through service and payment.

Village Study in Madhya Pradesh and Chhattisgarh

Madhya Pradesh occupied significant place in village study because it was a field of researches of two great social anthropologists. One great social anthropologist was A.C. Mayer of London School of Economics and other anthropologist was K.S. Mathur of Lucknow University.

These two anthropologists did researches in two different villages in the same period 1954-56 and published research papers and books. A.C. Mayer made study of Malwa village and published research papers and books on caste system and social change. In his book *Caste and Kinship in Central India* (1960), following the tradition of British Social Anthropology, Mayer attempted to describe the social structure of a Malwa village based on caste and kinship. The study was based on fieldwork in Ramkheri village located at a distance of 11 km from small town Devas on plateau of Malwa and 45 km from Ujjain. The village had a population of 912 persons distributed in 27 castes. Mayer was influenced by S.F. Naddel and C. von Furer Haimendorf in fieldwork and analysis of data. Mayer distinguished three types of membership in a caste. The lowest layer was of a sub-caste called kindered of cooperation. This varied for each individual at any time. Around this was a group called kindered of recognition within which marriages were made. This group was large and amorphous. It was same for members of sub-caste of a village. Beyond this, there were people which were recognised as a member of sub-caste but were endogamous separate from sub-castes. It was spread over a larger area and was not an effective group. From his study Mayer came to conclusion that it was sub-caste which was really endogamous and caste had no mechanism of settling disputes. Here, he was in full agreement with Srinivas that it was sub-caste which was endogamous and regarded by particular caste and individual, though caste was recognised by the society at large.

Mayer made a distinction between external and internal relation of a caste. The external relations existed within the village and internal relations existed on kinship relations in different villages. Here, Mayer seemed to be influenced by the concept of vertical caste solidarity and horizontal caste solidarity. Mayer also established caste hierarchy in Ramkheri on the basis of ritual criteria, rules of commensality and concept of purity and pollution.

The other book on Malwa village was written by K.S. Mathur, *Caste and Ritual in a Malwa Village* (1964). This book was based on study of a Malwa village Potlod. The fieldwork was sponsored by Australian National University and was written under the guidance of S.F. Nadal. Mathur conducted fieldwork in between April 1955 to April 1956. The village Potlod was located at a distance of 26 km south-west of Ujjain. It had a population of 1062 persons divided into 28 castes. He analysed the function of Hinduism in integration of caste society. On the basis of his researches Mathur described ritual status of castes. He established that fundamental feature of Hindu Social Organisation was caste and the entire system was bounded by notion of purity and pollution. The concept of purity and pollution was discussed at intra-caste and inter-caste relationships. Various types of purity and pollution were also analysed. Mathur examined the structural network of the village in relation to rituals which perpetuated the system of religious ideas and beliefs.

Village Studies in Rajasthan

G.M. Carstairs had made a study of Rajasthan village Deoli and published his book, *Twice-born: A Study of High Caste Hindus* (1957). He had undertaken the fieldwork in 1951-52 under the financial support of Rockfeller Foundation. He had taken this study in collaboration with Gital P. Steed. The study attempted to test certain hypotheses of personality development and character formation in a non-Western society where processes of socialization were different. For this purpose, the village Deoli was chosen. The village Deoli was located at foothills of Arawali range near Udaipur. The village had a population of 2417 persons distributed in 594 families and 36 castes. In course of fieldwork, certain psychological tests such as Raven's professive matrices tests and Rorschach tests. In addition to in-depth interviews, 45 case studies were taken from 13 Rajputs, 11 Brahmins, and nine Muslims on the basis of field data and psychological tests analysis. Carstairs made generalised statement regarding personality structure of High Caste Hindus. According to him, Rajputs being martial community, emphasized on authority, and wider personal fortitude, pride and self-assertions. They were supposed to take life, keep concubine, drink alcohol and eat meat. Banias of the village subscribed Hinduism but emphasized on wealth above everything. The great majority of Banias of the village tempered their materialism with philanthropic and religious deeds.

Carstairs had considered the influences of socialisation on personality formation of High Caste Hindus of Deoli. According to him personality formation was influenced by two sources: (i) Individual biological inheritance, and (ii) learning experiences. In discussing the unconscious process of formation of national character in Hindus, he assumed that events of early stages of human psychological maturation had an enduring influence throughout the later life and led to the formation of national character. According to him, the basic personality structure of High Caste Hindus was identified as paranoidic, suspiciousness, egocentricity and reluctance to make transient relationship. They had greatest self-assurance in formal etiquette. The people displayed an apparent lack of sympathy for each other sexual appetite which was suppressed as much as possible. Village showed tolerance and goodwill. Taken together, the study was unique, inspiring and opened up a new area of research in caste system prevalent in Indian villages. His microscopic approach to understand national character of three high caste Hindus—Rajput, Brahmin and Bania, was subjected to criticism also. The claim of author about national character was partial because it was concerned with only three high castes of a Rajasthan village.

Carstairs had published a research paper under the title, "Patterns of Religious Observance in Three Villages of Rajasthan" (1961). He studied the religious practice of three villages of Rajasthan. This paper was based on one and half months field-work in the village Sujarapa in early months of 1950. He tried to examine continuum from Bhil tribals at one hand and peasant culture with many Sanskritic elements on the other hand in the sphere of religion. In showing similarities and differences among three representative villages, the gradual process of Hinduization and Sanskritisation was indicated not in temporal but in spatial perspective. He brought out the presence of both great and little traditions in village religion, but did not deal with process of interaction.

Another scholar B.R. Chauhan studied a village Sadari. The village Sadari was located in Chittorgarh district of Rajasthan. This village had a population of 640 persons distributed in 130 families. The village was inhabited by Rajput, Bhil, Gadari, and other castes. In the background of rich ethnographic data, Chauhan established that village was characterised by smallness and distinctiveness in the sphere of rituals, festivals, and village deity. It was not so homogeneous as a caste. The village was not self-sufficient. But it could be viewed as a whole. It had its own identity.

On the basis of study of Sadari village, Chauhan criticized the concept of peasant society, because it dealt with only a section of villagers dependent on agriculture and brought to focus only the economic aspect of the village. In place of peasant society, he considered the concept of little community more appropriate and acceptable because of holistic concept of community. He pointed out the villagers had various kinds of linkages with outside world. He has talked about traditional linkages of the village and modern linkages of the village.

B.R. Chauhan had also encouraged a number of his students to undertake village study in Rajasthan. Yogesh Atal, one of his students, made a valuable study of caste system of a Mewar village in Rajasthan. Based on this study, he published a research paper entitled, "Cult of Bheru in a Mewar Village" (1961). He studied a Mewar village from the point of view of deity and worship. He found the prevalence of Bheru cult in Mewar. He made a comparative study of Bheru worship reported by A.C. Mayer in Mewar village. Unlike in Malwa, in the Shrine Bheru in Mewar was a centre of corporate worship. In Malwa, Bheru was a lineage deity, but in Mewar Bheru was a village deity and had inter-village significance.

Since the cult of Bheru had Brahminical and non-Brahminical attributes and rituals, it was difficult to apprehend whether Bhairava of great tradition was a universalized version of Bheru or Bheru is a parochialized form of Bhairava. Atal considered that it was a parochially universalized form and mode of worship was more significant than universalized traits. He found that in Malwa and Rajasthan, the process of universalization had followed different paths. According to him, Bheru worship was not reported from north India, hence it was a local deity; and Bheru and Bhairava were two different deities with only resemblance in name. Concept of universalization and univerzalization developed by McKim Marriott were also utilized here for analysing the cult Bheru with Bhairava of great tradition. But, he had synthesized the concepts of universalisation and parochialisation in one term parochially universalized. But in absence of any definition and clarification, the concept remained functional and vague.

Village Study in Gujarat

Geital P. Sleed, a scholar of Columbia University, made a study of village Kasandra along with a research team of four American and three Indian scholars. The village Kasandra was located in Sanad Taluka in Ahmedabad district of Gujarat. It was located at a distance of 54 km from Ahmedabad city. The village had a population of 850 persons and was studied in between November 1949 and January 1951. In his long paper, "Personality formation in Hindu Villages in Gujarat" (1955), Geital P. Sleed attempted to formulate an approach for the study of personality formation in a Gujarat village. At first level approach was stated theoretically and then documented with evidence at two levels—sociological and ontogenetic. In the background of socio-psychological data, the ideal virtues and value orientation of Rajputs were discussed at the axis of self. The community was examined from the point of view of good life and changes in personality structures in context of changing social norms in village.

Another scholar T.B. Nayak made study of four groups of Pattidars and dealt with their social structure in his paper, "Social Status in Gujarat" (1957).

A.M. Shah and R.G. Shroff studied Vahirvanca Barots of Gujarat and wrote a paper, "Vahirvanca Barots of Gujarat" (1958). In this paper, they have brought out the roles of the community of geneologists and mythographers who operated in rural Gujarat.

Village Study in Maharashtra

In Maharashtra, Henry Orenstein made study of a village named Gaon in Poona district in 1954-55 and during summer of 1961. The village Gaon was located at a distance of 2 km from market town Mot. It was inhabited by 14 castes. At the time of study the dominant caste of the village was Dhangar. They were traditionally shepherd but now they had become Rajput. In the light of these field data, Orenstein wrote papers, "Leadership and Caste in Bombay Village" (1959) and "Caste and Welfare State" (1963). In these papers, he discussed the functioning and ranking of castes as well as the village social structure and ritual system. Based on study of the Gaon village, he published a book *Gaon: Conflict and Cohesion* (1965). In this book, he had tried to establish that the nature of caste system was undergoing changes.

Processes of Sanskritisation, Westernisation and modernization were responsible for changes in caste system.

G.S. Ghurye did fieldwork in village Haweli Taluka during four seasons in 1954-1958 and published a book *After a Century and Quarter* (1960). The purpose of study was two-fold—(i) To test the concept of folk urban continuum, and (ii) to bring out changes in the village life. Ghurye with his vast learning in ancient Hindu scriptures gave historical perspective of the village community and presented a comparative picture of changes in the village that had occurred since 1819. The year 1819 was taken as a base year because this village was studied by Major Coats in 1819. This was restudied by Ghurye after a century and quarter. That is why the title of the book was given as *After a Century and a Quarter*. In the book, unity of the village was demonstrated by working of village council, common shrines and their mutual participation in festivals of the village. But the picture of the village life was incomplete. Many topics such as Baluta system, life cycle, caste structure and kinship systems were not touched. He attempted to show local community as an integrated whole, but he failed to do so in absence of adequate field materials.

The next book of Ghurye was under the title, *Anatomy of Rural-Urban Community* (1963). It was based on pilot study of whole Haweli Taluka in Maharashtra. The fieldwork was carried out for three months each year 1954-1960 by research assistants. In total 117 villages were surveyed in which there were 8 agricultural towns, 9 super villages, 34 big villages, 39 standard villages and 29 small villages. The study was undertaken with a view to show rural-urban continuum to help welfare agencies and facilitate industrialization. Although the book was dominated by statistical analysis, but provided description about socio-religious and socio-economic aspects of village life of different caste communities with urbanizing influences. Ghurye was successful in carrying out such a large scale anthropological survey, which was rare at that time in India.

Village Study in Andhra Pradesh

In Andhra Pradesh S.C. Dube studied a village Shamirpet in the region of Telangana, now a separate state and published a first full length monograph under the title "Indian Village" (1955). This book is based on fieldwork at Shamirpet village with the help of five research investigators. The author was further assisted by five other faculty units which did social work in the village in their special areas of interest and technical competence. This interdisciplinary collaboration was sponsored and financed by Social Service Extension Project of Osmania University in 1951-52. Professor S.C. Dube was Director of this project.

The village Shamirpet was located at a distance of 40 km from Hyderabad and had a population of 2494 persons including 340 Muslims. There were 15 different Hindu castes in the village. In the light of field data an integrated picture of the village was presented and historical, geographical and sociological perspectives were taken care of adequately. The foreword of the book was written by Morris Edward Opler. He in the foreword of the book observed that it was a solid study which would doubtlessly take its place among the standard community studies made in various parts of the world. He further observed that in a number of ways this volume was specially valuable and challenging and was a tonic to present day research in Indian village life.

Although it was one of the earliest monographs on a village, but it presented a comprehensive picture of functioning of village institutions. Dube noted that the economic system of rural India was founded on the caste's functional specialisation, interdependence and occupational mobility. He also noted that elements of classical Hinduism of an all-India spread were mingled with regional beliefs and practices of Hindus of Deccan plateau. Three major types of religious beliefs and practices were observed in the village—(i) Family ceremonies, (ii) Village ceremonies and (iii) Caste ceremonies. Muslims had their own familial and communal festivals. The Hindus and the Muslims interacted with each other on common village festivals.

Dube gave a short account of worldview, inter-group relation, inter-caste attitudes and stereotypes and discussed the three most significant stages of life—childhood, youthhood and oldhood in a generalised biography.

In addition to this full length study *Indian Village* (1955), Dube wrote few papers based on village study. His paper entitled, "Ranking of Caste in Telangana village" (1955), was published in *Rural Profile of India* edited by D.N. Majumdar (1955). According to Dube, the fundamental principle of caste ranking in Shamirpet was also determined by traditions and myths, because caste was based on ascribed system of status. He also established that the observance of prescribed daily rituals, hierarchy of food eaten, occupations allowed and practised and observance of rules connected with life cycle rituals determined caste rank. He was of opinion that the only criteria for caste ranking in villages were rituals and not economic. Srinivas in his study of "Coorgs of South India" had demonstrated that economic dominance of a group led to ritual rationalization of high status. Marriott also suggested that castes were ranked on the basis of interaction among them instead of attributes.

T.R. Singh, a student of Dube, wrote a dissertation on the Madigas of Andhra Pradesh and published a paper on "Hierarchy of Deities in an Andhra Village" (1961). This paper was based on the study of village Madhawaram located at a distance of 22 km from Hyderabad. The village had a population of 500 persons distributed in 17 castes and 4 semi-tribal groups. Singh attempted a hierarchy of deities on the basis of six criteria:

- Attributes, power and virtue of a deity.
- Food offering acceptable to a deity.
- Observance of fast in honour of deity.
- Trance and dance in honour of a deity.
- Types of priest worshipping a deity.
- The spread of worship of a deity.

Although hierarchy of deity according to different criteria was given, but an overall ranking was not developed. The parochial and universal nature of these deities was not clear. They had both, Brahminical and non-Brahminical attributes. The caste hierarchy presented was not correlated to hierarchy of deities. However, the study provided a refreshing perspective and a significant approach to the study of religion in a village.

After S.C. Dube, Y.V. Lakshmana Rao published his book on studies of two villages of Andhra Pradesh. One village was Katharu and the other village was Potharu. The meaning of Katharu in Telugu is new, on account of more progressive character of its residents and being more industrialized and developed than its counterpart Potharu. The meaning of Potharu in Telugu is old on account of its more traditional character.

The title of the book was *Communication and Development:*

A Study of Two Indian Villages (1972). In this book, Rao was mainly concerned with relationship between communication and development. According to him, changes in Kotharu were consequence of increased flow of communication. It had made the people of Kotharu aware of alternative way of earning a livelihood and promoted the diversification of their economic pursuit. In the social sphere also communication had to breakdown the old caste prejudices and practices. On the basis of facts and statistics collected from Kotharu and Potharu villages of Andhra Pradesh, Rao made a simple and straightforward conclusion. He opined that communication familiarized villagers with new and alternative ways of earning a livelihood, reduced pressure on land, created demand for goods, encouraged local initiative to meet those demands, enlarged the entrepreneurial base, increased a shift from heredity to achievement, as status criteria and promoted accumulative acceleration of economic growth. Socially and politically, Rao showed that communication reduced the elite mass gap, promoted equalitarian idea, encouraged breakdown of old caste prejudice and increased political participation. According to Rao, local and regional developmental programmes should be based on need of an area.

Another scholar Paul G. Herbert made study of a large village Konduru and published his book under the title *Konduru: Structure and Integration in a South Indian Village* (1971). The village Konduru was located in Nallamallac Hills south-west of city of Hyderabad. He had described social and political organisation of an Andhra village. Based on three years of fieldwork, Herbert presented a holistic picture of quality of life in Konduru and made this monograph an excellent introduction to social and political organization of Indian village and regions. At few places Herbert referred to leather workers and Panchalas as left-hand castes, but there were no reference to right-hand castes. But he failed to elaborate these categorisation which was dealt with by Brenda E.F Beck in his book *Peasant Society in Konku : A Study of Left and Right Sub-castes in South India* (1972).

Village Study in Karnataka

The state of Karnataka occupies significant place in India so far as village study was concerned. Here village studies were conducted by scholars like Dhillon, Srinivas, Beals,

McCormack, Epstein, Ishwaran and Harper. They had contributed a lot in the study of village in India in general and Mysore in particular. Dhillon studied a village Haripura in Malvali Taluka in Mandya district of Mysore state. The study was undertaken under the auspices of Programme Evaluation Organisation of Planning Commission on the same pattern as the study of Rampura near Delhi by Oscar Lewis. On the basis of his study, Dhillon published a book under the title, *Leadership and Groups in a South Indian Village* (1955). In this book, Dhillon attempted to highlight the prevalence of facts and leadership pattern in an Indian village. Here attempt was made to a comparison between north Indian village Rampura and South Indian village Haripura. According to him, the village Haripura had more tolerant and peaceful atmosphere than the north Indian village Rampura studied by Lewis. Unlike a north Indian village, the position of women in Haripura was high. The marital relation was confined largely within the circle of few villages. 21 per cent marriages were held within the village itself. This factor weakened factional network from spreading and reduced the rigidity of factional behaviour. As Haripura was a mono caste village, faction along caste and kinship ties was not an important factor. The leadership in the village was not symbolized by one or two individuals but a group having their own leadership. Factors contributing to leadership were economic and social status of family. The individual personality traits such as education, enterprise and innovation were less important than traditional and conservative factors. The study was significant because it revealed that village pattern described by Oscar Lewis in North Indian village was not similar to South Indian village. Again, kinship was a less important factor for factions in a South Indian village.

Mysore was a veritable laboratory for social anthropological researches for M.N. Srinivas. He studied a village Rampura for 10 months in 1948 and paid several visits in the village time to time. The village was located at a distance of 40 km south-east of Mysore city. The village had a population of 1523 persons at the time of study. On the basis of this study, Srinivas wrote his first doctoral dissertation on social organisation of Mysore families and then religion and society among Coorgs of South India at Oxford University. This was published in the form of book in

1952. In this book, he postulated the concept of Sanskritisation and vertical and horizontal unity in the village. According to him, Sanskritisation is a process by which, a member of low caste adopted the lifeways of high castes particularly Brahmins. He called this process of change as Sanskritisation. For example, performing bath in morning, putting *Tilak* on forehead, wearing *Janeu* (sacred thread), offering water to Sun-God and *Tulsi* plant, reciting hymns, visiting to temples for worship, giving up non-vegetarian food and sharing breakfast after worship. By following such lifeways, a member of low caste did not claim as Brahmin, but he showed their position higher than those members of own castes who did not follow such lifeways. Srinivas called this as Brahmanical model of change in Hindu society. Later on, he added Kshatriya and Vaishya model of Sanskritisation. He also postulated the concept of desanskritisation for adopting the life-ways of low caste Hindus by high caste Hindus. For example, taking non-vegetarian food and wine and not performing daily bath and worship before breakfast. At Oxford University, Srinivas was influenced by the concept of social structure developed by A.R. Radcliffe-Brown. Under his influence, he made study of social system of Rampura such as relationship of roles and status and castes and their occupation. He wrote a paper on "Social System of a Mysore Village" which was published in McKim Marriott's edited book *Village India* (1955). In this paper, Srinivas emphasized on unity of the village. He observed that village was a vertical entity made up of several horizontal layers each of which was a caste. The unity of the village was expressed by village officials supervising the rituals, village elders and the dominant caste.

In his another paper, "The Dominant Caste in Rampura" (1959), he attempted to clarify and redefine the concept of dominant caste on the basis of Rampura study and documents of disputes in inter-village Panchayat organisation. According to him, the most important elements of dominance were as follows:

- Numerical preponderance
- Economic and political power
- A high ritual status
- Western education
- Occupation.

A.R. Beals studied two villages of Mysore, namely Namhali and Gopalpur. The village Namhali was located near Bangalore city. The investigation was carried out in 1952-53 for 15 months. The purpose was to describe the history of external factors changing the social structure of the village since 1800. The village Gopalpur was located in Yadgiri Tehsil of Mysore state. He studied the village with his wife in 1959-60. On the basis of this study of Namhali, Beals presented a doctoral dissertation "Cultural Change and Social Conflict in a South Indian Village" at University of California in 1954. Although this thesis was not published but in a long research paper, "Inter-play among Factors of Change in a Mysore Village", published in the book *Village India* edited by McKim-Marriott (1955), he brought out six factors responsible for the growth of village. They were as follows:

- Trade and commerce
- Increasing population
- Communication and manufacture
- State-wide Government
- Education
- Money economy.

Here, changes were shown through external factors. Variations in different strata of village society were not considered in dealing with change. Internal factors of change were equally important. But, he unfortunately ignored the caste, class and family distinction in assessing the nature and direction of change.

In his another paper, "Leadership in a Mysore Village" (1959), he analysed the impact of increasing urbanization on village leadership. The traditional pattern of leadership was in process of disintegration, new factions started dominating the village leadership.

Based on study of Gopalpur village, Beals published a book *Gopalpur: A South Indian Village* (1962). He attempted to describe the insider's view of villages. Castes in the village Gopalpur were ranked according to hierarchy as per ritual criteria, food consumption and traditional occupation. These were placed on a scale of purity and pollution. He noted a correlation between caste and class. The position of Brahmins was high because they worshipped a hierarchy of Gods. The Gods like Shiva and Basawa were worshipped by high castes and vegetarian Brahmin priest. The lower god Hanumanata was worshipped by most of the villagers during community-based festivals. The non-vegetarian Gods and Goddesses were worshipped by low castes. They were concerned with practical needs of villagers. The village life was marked by fairs and festivals. After every 28 days a village-wide ceremony was performed. In these ceremonies representation of each caste had a special role. The ceremonies were participated by all villagers.

An American scholar W. McCormack studied two villages—Morsvalli and Huillipanhalli. The village Morsvalli had a population of 504 persons and the village Huillipanhalli had a population of 252 persons. Both villages were near Bangalore in Mysore state. Based on fieldwork in these two villages, he wrote two research papers. His first research paper was "Sister's Daughters Marriage in a Mysore Village" (1953) and his second research paper was, "Factionalism in Mysore Village" (1959). In his first paper he attempted to explore sister's daughters marriage on the basis of kinship terminology. In his second paper, he attempted to show that the power of traditional leadership had declined in the village for three reasons—(i) Secularisation, (ii) Doubt about neutrality and good character of some village elders, and (iii) Personal interest of village leaders in village disputes. He also recorded the increase of factional leadership owing to operation of several external factors.

Another scholar E.B. Harper did field researches at Totagadal in Malnad of Mysore state. He with his wife stayed in village from November 1954 to February 1956. He wrote two papers on the basis of his fieldwork. His first research paper was "Two Systems of Economic Exchange in Village India" (1959) and his second research paper was "Political Organisation and Leadership in Karnataka Village". In his first paper he discovered the pattern of *Jajmani* system prevalent in Totagadi village of Mysore state. Here, he discovered two types of economic transaction—(i) The *Jajmani* system of traditional nature, and (ii) The Malnad system which occurred between the *Jajman* and artisans for extra work. The Malnad system had cash transaction and the *Jajmani* system had kind transaction. He found that *Jajmani* system was disintegrating into Malnad type of economic relation in Indian villages.

In his another paper Harper examined the position and role of dominant caste namely Havik Brahmins in the same village. He further examined the dynamics of village leadership, feuds, factions and role of parties in decision-making. He concluded that the village retained its traditions in the form of leadership and process of decision-making. Individual Havik Brahmins were major leaders, they played role in strengthening or weakening the position of a non-Brahmin leader.

A British scholar Scarlett Epstein carried out fieldwork in two villages—Wangala and Donela for two years between 1954-56. Wangala was an irrigated village and Donela was an unirrigated village. The Wangala was located at a distance of 8 kms from Mandala and was a multi-caste village of 192 households. She wrote few papers and later a book on the basis of study of these villages.

In her first paper, "A Sociological Analysis of Witch Beliefs in a Mysore Village" (1959), she made analysis of witch beliefs sociologically. The witch beliefs were common in the village society. It was related to superstition and fear in the name of witch. In her second paper "Economic Development and Peasant Marriage" (1960), she described that economic development among peasant had brought changes in the marriage of peasant society. Her book, *Economic Development and Social Change* (1962), was significant because it was a first full-length village study in Mysore region and written by a such scholar who was anthropologist as well as economist. In this book, the author made an attempt to highlight the impact of irrigation on social and economic organisation of the village within the regional economy. In the analysis of structural change, she established a positive relation between economic, organisational and ritual change. The economic change was determining valuable. The persistence of economic and social values had delayed social change. She had made a limited comparison between irrigated village Wangala with unirrigated village Donela.

K. Ishwaran made an intensive study of village Shivapura near Dharwar and published two books under the title, *Tradition and Economy in Village India* (1966) and *Shivapura: A South Indian Village* (1968). In his first book *Tradition and Economy in Village India,* he described the traditional economic activities of villagers. He attempted to discuss social structure, Aya and caste, rights and responsibilities, strength and values, conflict and tensions and evaluation. In this way, he focused attention on economic aspects of the village in framework of social context.

Ishwaran in his first book proposed to formulate sociology of exchange. Aya explain the exchange of society. According to him, Aya is unmeasured and unconditional gift and reflects the motif of sharing one's possessions with others. In the legal sphere, traditional Aya system recognises rights of individuals, groups and of community in the sphere of politics. The *Jajmans* whether of street, caste or village, get leadership and headship automatically. The author finds a very close correspondence of Aya system in the Potlach institution of Polynesia, Kwakiukl, Kula exchange of Trobri and islanders and so on.

Ishwaran's next book *Shivapura: A South Indian Village* (1968) is based upon the study of same village located at a distance of two miles from the city of Dharwar and ten miles from Hubli. The village contained a wide range of caste Lingyatas, Marhattas and Muslims. In a monographic style, Ishwaran described styles of life of various caste groups and concentrated on inter-caste and inter-village relationship. He referred to the solidarity within the village as well as inter-village cooperation. While describing the religious beliefs and practice of villages, he termed religion as an integrating force.

K. Ishwaran's third book *Change and Continuity in India's Village* (1970) is an edited book. It contains 10 papers contributed by American and British anthropologists on different aspects of village life. The book examined the continuity and traditions and changes brought by modernisation in Indian villages. In this edited volume, a long paper was contributed by Alan Beals under the title, "Village Life in South India" (1974). Based on some field material supplemented by short visits during 1953-1966, Beals made valuable contribution to the study of South Indian villages. In the light of materials from three villages of Mysore, namely Namhalli, Elephant and Gopalpur, Beals emphasized the relationships between villages and their surroundings. Following an ecological approach, he described the ecosystem of the village as an interaction between the cultural tradition of a set of people and their environment. In an analytical manner, Beals described the ecological basis of economy, technology, the network of intra- and inter-village relationships and, thus, presented a model to understand village life in south Indian villages. Beals used frequently, the south Indian civilization, which was not accepted by Milton, Singer and Raghavan. According to them, south Indian villages are part of greater network of Indian civilization and channels of communication between past and present have been quite effective between North and South India.

Village Study in Kerala and Tamil Nadu

In Kerala and Tamil Nadu village studies remained neglected. Although a study of tribes of Travancore and Kochin was initiated by noted scholar Anand Krishna Ayer in early twenties which was later followed by communities study of Andre Mayer and Kathleen Gough.

A.C. Mayer on the basis of village studies in Malabar, wrote a book, *Land and Society in Malabar* (1974). In this book, he described the village society of Malabar region. He also wrote a paper, "Change in Malabar Village" (1955). In this paper, he had described the changes occurring in Malabar village due to contact with urban centres and democratic institutions.

Gough studied three villages of Kerala during 1947-49 and published papers on village life in Kerala. In her first paper, "Criteria of Caste Ranking" (1950), Gough described social and ritual criteria of caste ranking prevalent in Kerala villages. In her second paper, "Social Structure of a Tanjore Village" (1955), she described family, marriage and kinship system and related institutions in a Tanjore village. In her third paper, "Cult of Dead Among Nayars" (1958), Gough described the cult of dead among Nayars.

On the basis of study of three villages of Malabar Coast and two villages of Tanjore of Tamil Nadu, Gough wrote about the social structure, kinship system, caste organisation and caste ranking in the village. She had studied one Brahmin village Kumbapettai, 12 km south-west of Tanjore town during 1951-52. The village had 12 castes. She noted a considerable changes in the traditional social structure of the village. The village was relatively isolated. Closed stationary system with a traditional intercaste relationship had moved half way in transition from relatively static feudal sub-system economy to a much wider expanding capitalist economy. The breakdown of feudal economic system, the emergence of lower caste groups in economic rivalry rather than cooperation and widening range of social relation outside the village had endangered at the power of Brahmins and unity of the village. Kinship ties within and between villages were gradually weakened by increasing heterogeneity of wealth, education and occupation.

The castes of Kumbapettai village were categorized into three classes: Brahmins, non-Brahmins and Adi Dravids. The spatial distribution of castes was corresponded to their occupational specialisation and mutual ritual rank. The traditional economy of caste was changing into modern economy due to government regulations, immigrations, urban employment and caste free occupation.

An another significant work was undertaken by Dagbin Sivertsen of Oslo University. He studied a village Thyaga Samuthiram located at a distance of 10 km from Kumbakonam, the largest town of Tanjore district of Madras state. The population of the village was 786 persons distributed in 10 castes. Brahmins had numerical dominance. The village was located on the bank of Kaveri river. Fieldwork was conducted from January 1956 to January 1958. He wrote a paper entitled, "When the Caste Barriers Fall: A Study of Social and Economic Change in South Indian Village" (1962). He presented the analysis of caste system, ritual order, inter-caste services, economy and system of cultivation, temple assemblage, village council and modern political movement. He brought out the weakening of traditionally privileged castes and economic and political advancement of subordinate castes. Describing the change in temple organisation, he described temple assemblage of each caste with elected headman or leaders as important agents of political control whose loyalties were being claimed by new associations. He emphasized that the economic system was primary determinant of fall of castes and rise of new political leaders. In the dynamics of caste system, the conflict between high castes and low castes was highlighted.

A full length study of Tanjore village was published by Andre Beteille. He studied a multi-caste village Shivpuram in Tanjore district. The village was located on the bank of river Kaveri had 92 Brahmins, 118 non-Brahmins, and 89 Adi Dravida householders living in separate areas.

Characteristics of Indian Villages

On the basis of village studies made in different states of India by American, British and Indian anthropologists, following characteristics of Indian villages have emerged:

- Indian villages are an integrated part of larger Indian society.
- Indian villages are strong examples of unity and extension.
- The tradition of villages is little and the tradition of town is great.
- But the little tradition and great tradition are not in isolation. They are interdependent, interrelated and interactive.
- Indian villages present a continuum between village and town.
- In Indian villages, there is parochialization of great tradition and in towns there are universalisation of little tradition.
- Each Indian village has its own boundary and acreage.
- Monoethnic caste village is rare in India. Majority villages are multi-caste village.
- In multi-caste village, each caste families live in a separate *Tola*.
- In villages main means of livelihood is agriculture and allied work.
- In villages land is not owned equally by all castes and families.
- Some families owned land and some families do not have land.
- Artisan castes provide their services to agriculturists.
- In Indian villages, *Jajmani* system is found in which different castes are tied socially and economically. The payment is made in kind.
- Indian villages are not self-dependant. They are related to other villages, towns, metropolises and national culture.
- Indian villages have concept of dominant castes; on the basis of numerical strength, high religious status, possessing land in the village and political power, education and money.

- In villages, social control is maintained by traditional village panchayats.
- In villages, there is existence of caste panchayat at regional level.
- Caste system is found in Indian villages.
- Caste system shows hierarchy and the concept of purity and pollution.
- Each village has its own history and village deities.
- In villages, festivals are celebrated collectively.
- Some caste festivals are also celebrated in the village.
- North Indian villages practice village exogamy rule, but in South Indian village exogamy rule is not followed.
- Indian villages are changing due to urbanisation, secularisation, modernisation and Sanskritisation, village development programmes and democratic institutions.
- Change processes have weakened traditional caste system, untouchability, concept of purity and pollution, traditional occupation, power structure and dominant caste concept.
- Factions and feuds are prevalent in Indian villages. Modern Gram Panchayat elections and community development programmes have increased factions, feuds and tensions in the village.

Major Contribution of Village Study

The major contribution of village studies are as follows:

- Village studies have helped in providing guidelines for community development programmes.
- Through village studies, anthropologists were able to formulate and field test methodology, concept and theories related to Indian villages.
- Indian villages got identity as a little unit of Indian civilization.
- A number of concepts such as Sanskritisation, urbanisation, little tradition, great tradition, universalisation, parochialisation, unity and extension, rural cosmopolitanism, dominant-caste, peasant-urban continuum, sacred complex,

Westernisation, modernisation, and caste mobility were propounded and field tested in the context of Indian villages.

- A number of scholars from America and Britain came to India to study Indian villages and characteristics of Indian villages was brought before world community.
- In the year 1955, three books on village study, *Indian Village* by S.C. Dube, *Village India* by McKim Marriott and *India's Village* by M.N. Srinivas were published. These books are still valuable for village study in India.

4
Caste Studies in India

Caste and caste system are identifying elements in Indian society. The caste and caste system have attracted the attention of scholars like Indologists, social anthropologists and sociologists. They have made study of castes and caste system from different angles. The number of books and papers published on castes and caste system is nearly 6000. B.N. Verma in his edited book *Contemporary India* (1964), attempted to divide the reviews of caste studies in three broad divisions on the basis of methodological approaches. They were as follows:

- Classical scriptural
- Cultural-Anthropological
- Sociological.

The classical scriptural view takes its clues from Vedas, Brahmanas, Puranas, Smritis and Hindu religious mythology regarding origin, purpose and destiny of caste system.

The cultural-anthropological studies of castes are an attempt to understand the organisational, structural, institutional and relational aspects of caste system.

The sociological studies approach the nature of caste system in terms of concept, social differentiation and stratification. Thus, in sociological tradition caste is viewed as a corporate entity, or as a principle of stratification and differentation of social order.

A.C. Sinha in his research paper, "Caste in India: Its Essential Patterns of Socio-cultural Integration" (1967), suggested to make study of castes and caste system applying anthropological and sociological approaches together. According to him, caste system has culture as well as structure both. Therefore, caste system involves anthropological and sociological approaches both. The caste should not be confused with race. Because there is a great difference between caste stratification and racial stratification.

L.P. Vidyarthi in his book, *Rise of Indian Anthropology*, Volume-2 (1978) attempted to present the caste studies in India through three stages, which were as follows:

- Formulatory stage (1974-1919)
- Constructive stage (1920-1949)
- Analytical stage (1950 onwards).

Caste Studies in Formulatory Stage

In the Formulatory Stage many handbooks on tribes and castes were published. Rev. M.A. Sherring published three books on Hindu tribes and castes in 1879. In the first volume tribes and castes of Benaras (Varanasi) were described. In the second volume, tribes and castes of Punjab and North-western province were described. In the third volume, tribes and castes of Presidency of Bombay and province of Sindh were described. These volumes by Sherring describe in brief social customs, religious beliefs and practices of different tribes and castes, living in those provinces. Sherring's efforts were followed by organised scheme of writing handbooks by several competent and scholarly administrators. They were as follows:

- Herbert Risley published his book *Tribes and Castes of Bengal* (1861).
- W. Crooke published his book *The Tribes and Castes of North Western Province and Oudh* (1896) (4 Volumes).
- R.V. Russel and Rai Bahadur Hira Lal published their book *Tribes and Castes of Central Province* (4 Volumes—1866).
- E. Thruston published his book, *Caste and Tribes of South India* (7 Volumes—1909).
- R.E. Thruston published his book *Tribes and Castes of Bombay* (3 Volumes—1920-22).
- L.K.A. Krishna Iyer published his book *Mysore Tribes and Castes* (4 Volumes—1924-25)
- L.K.A. Krishna Iyer published his book *Travancore Tribes and Castes* (1 Volume—1937).

Besides these scholarly administrators some scholars also attempted to study the caste and caste system which helped later scholars to formulate concepts and theories on caste and caste system.

Bhattacharya published his book, *Hindu Castes and Sects* (1896). In this book, he described different Hindu castes and sects prevalent in south and north India. An account of Brahmin caste, warrior caste, writer caste, trader caste and *shudra* caste were presented in the book.

T.M. Nathu Bhai's book *Hindu Caste, Ceremony, Custom and Inheritance* (1896) brought out religious beliefs, practices, marriage ritual, death ritual and inheritance pattern of Hindu castes.

Some army officers were also assigned duty of writing books by British Government on Indian castes and tribes. After 1857 revolt, army officers were entrusted to study the custom, tradition, beliefs and practices of different castes and tribes from the point of view of appointment in army. Army officer A.H. Bingley, and Captain A. Nicholls made study of Brahmin, Rajput, Jat, Gujar, Ahir castes and published book *Caste Handbook for Indian Army*. On Brahmin (1897), Rajput (1899) and Jat, Gujars and Ahirs (1904).

Army officer Mackenzie wrote a paper, "Customs of Komati caste" (1879). In this paper, he attempted to show various marriage customs prevalent in Komati caste and their relationship with Madiga caste.

From the point of view of social-cultural anthropology, earlier studies made by census commissioners and some scholars were of great value. Because they had thrown light on nature, origin, system and function of Indian castes and caste system. They had published their views in the form of books. Denzil Ibbetson published *Punjab Caste* (1916) and *Punjab Census Report* (1881). He propounded the occupational theory of caste and religious theory of caste for the first time. According to him, the diversity of caste was based on occupational diversity.

J.C. Nesfield in his book, *Brief View of Caste System of North Western Province and Oudh* (1885) opined that the present division of Indian people into caste was totally functional and occupational. There were one Indian race and one Indian caste.

Henry Herbert Risley who was Census Commissioner of Bengal, published his book, *The People of India* (1905) proposed racial and hypergamous theory of caste. According to him, the primary factor in the determination of caste was race. On the basis of anthropometric evidence, he identified seven physical types among Indian people and established a close relation between these seven racial types and seven distinct types of castes. He observed that castes varied in social rank according to the average nasal index of members. This racial theory of caste did not find support from ethnological basis of castes. According to him, certain correlation existed in race and caste in north India. Aboriginal priests had gained status as Brahmins and aboriginal chieftains as Kshatriya. Some tribes and foreign racial groups had also entered the pole of Hinduism and had become caste.

Another scholar M. Emile Senart in his book *Les Castes Dansi* (1896) propounded the genetic theory of caste. According to this French Orientalist, the Indian caste system was the normal development of ancient Aryan institutions like family, genes and tribe which corresponded respectively to family, clan and caste in India. He pointed out similarity between marriage restrictions in ancient Greece and Rome and Indian Caste endogamy and clan exogamy.

An Indian scholar S.V. Kettar published his book, *The History of Caste in India,* Part-I (1909) and Part-II (1911). Tracing the cultural history of India, Kettar attempted to establish that prior to the immigrations of Rigvedic Aryans, India was populated by many tribes belonging to many races including some Aryan tribes who preceded the Rigvedic Aryans. In course of time, in the upper valleys of Ganges, Brahmins evolved first of all as a caste and then as a sacerdotal caste. In course of time, Brahmins migrated in all parts of India and carried the idea of four *varnas*—Brahmin, Kshatriya, Vaishya and Shudra. They applied this idea to local condition elsewhere. According to him, the entire caste system was rested on notion of purity and pollution.

Another administrator scholar Edward Gate who in Census Report of India (1911) enumerated the factors that gave birth to caste system. He suggested that the present rigidity of caste restrictions among functional groups emerged owing to power exercised by caste panchayat. He pointed out that the final development of caste system would have not taken place in Punjab, which was occupied first by Aryan tribes, but further east possibly in kingdom of Magadh. According to him, caste was invention of Brahmins who had powerful voice in determining the relative ranks of castes. But they were not concerned with their internal affairs with the process of fusion and fission from which the caste of present day had evolved.

Constructive Phase

J.H. Hutton, Census Commissioner of India (1931), in his book *Caste in India* (1946) highlighted the origin of caste system in terms of *Mana* (spiritism). This book provided us basic information about structure and function of caste system in different parts of India. Hutton possessed encyclopaedic knowledge of existing literatures and field experience. He examined the emergence and development of caste system as an interaction of a number of geographical, social, political, religious and economic factors. He advocated the *Mana* principle in Buddhist religion as *Siddhi,* in Islamic beliefs as *Kudrat* and Hindu beliefs as *Sakti.* According to him, caste system was established by divine ordinance. He was of opinion that a number of factors contributed in the emergence and development of case system. They were as follows:

- Geographical isolation of Indian peninsula as a whole and individual areas within it.
- Primitive ideas about power of food to transmit qualities.
- Similar ideas of totemism, taboo, *mana* and soul stuff or life matter.
- Ideas of pollution, ablution, purification and ceremonial purity in association with ritual sacrifices.
- Ideas of exclusive family, ancestor worship and sacramental meal.
- Belief in magic associated with craft function.
- Hereditary occupations and trade craft secrets.
- Guilds and association of that character and various factors in development of economic life.
- Clash and antagonistic culture—matrilineal and patrilineal cultures.
- Clash of races, colour prejudice and consequent social and religious practices—privileges.
- Individual isolation of tribes and policies of their inclusion without absorption into larger administrative units.
- Delicate economic and administrative policies.
- Exploitation by highly intelligent hierarchy.

E.A.H. Blunt wrote his book on *Caste System of North India* (1931). He described endogamy as essential principle of caste and Brahmin hegemony as threat of unity. According to him, commensal restrictions were result of animistic taboos reinforced by Brahminical doctrine of ceremonial purity. The book of Blunt was based on several census volumes on castes and Crook's work was based on *Tribes and Castes of North-western Province and Oudh*. Blunt gave us a full account of origin and evolution of caste system, the nature of customs common to all castes, principles of such customs, and reasons for similarity and differences in caste. In a series of 16 chapters, origin, evolution, nature, function, types, interrelatedness and future of caste system were discussed clearly. Although each chapter was significant and rich in terms of presentation, but discussion on various types of castes such as sectarian caste, hill caste, gypsy caste, Muslim caste, and new caste occupied special significance.

N.K. Dutta in his voluminous book, *Origin and Growth of Caste in India* (1931) provided a detailed description of origin and growth of caste system in India. According to him, the major factor of origin of caste system in India was a battle between Aryans and non-Aryans. Due to division of labour in society, caste system originated. Non-Aryans did not have division of labour. The highest position of priest, witch doctor and hereditary occupation were also responsible for origin of caste system.

Dutta observed that some of seeds of castes were common to the stock of Aryan people in all countries, but they failed to grow elsewhere. They found a more fertile soil in India due to absence of strong political power during Vedic and Epic Ages. The Aryan crushed tribal differences and enforced uniform law and custom because of cosmopolitanism of Indian religion which failed to draw a distinction between Indian and foreign religion. The book of Dutta provided many earlier theories of origin of caste system and did not throw any new light on the subject. But he succeeded in giving a comprehensive history based on ancient sacred writings for the development of caste system.

The most authentic theory of caste was propounded by G.S. Ghurye in his book, *Caste and Race in India* (1932). He proposed the Aryan theory of caste and substantiated it with numerous documents.

G.W. Briggs based on Census of 1911 published a book *The*

Chamars (1920). This was a first book in which description about a particular caste was presented.

W.H. Wiser in his book, *Hindu Jajmani System* (1936) gave description of *Jajmani* system which had held together agriculturists, artisans and other castes since centuries. This was a socio-economic system prevalent among different castes for service and payment in kind.

Among the French sociologists, the contribution of Celestin Bougle for understanding the origin, development and effect of caste system deserved special mention. He wrote his book, in Franch *Essais Sur le Regime des lastes* (Bibliotheque de Philosophic Contemporains) (1935). This book was translated in English by D.F. Pock under the title *Indian Caste System* (1971). This book of Bougle provided material on caste system and social stratification to the French laymen. The book had become the source of inspiration for two French sociologists—A.M. Hocart and Luis Dumont. Bougle had identified three essential features of caste. They were: hereditary specialisation, hierarchy and mutual repulsion. He opined that the spirit of caste united these three tendencies. He was of the opinion that without considering these three tendencies, one could not define a caste and understand the caste system. His concept of repulsion encompasses all those features by means of which each caste attempted to maintain distinctiveness and separation from other caste including commensal and connubial restriction.

Caste Study in Analytical Phase

The analytical period of caste study in Indian social anthropology marked the beginning of empirical studies of caste in India. With the interest in village studies of caste in India. With the interest in village studies, empirical and analytical study of caste system operating in Indian Villages become popular among anthropologists. To American, British, French and Indian scholars who undertook the study of villages in different parts of India, caste system provided a common cultural idiom. Social anthropologists like D.N. Majumdar, S.C. Dube, M.N. Srinivas, Iravati Karve, Oscar Lewis, Milton Singer, McKim Marriott, A.C. Mayer, B.S. Cohn, S.K. Mathur and others attempted to understand the village organisation in terms of caste organisation; caste dynamics, caste interactions and inter-caste relations. Caste factions and feuds were also studied. Such studies which became fashionable during analytical period since 1949 onwards, have been presented and discussed in Chapter-3 under the title *Village Studies in India*. Hence, we are not going to repeat them again here. Readers are requested to study the chapter three materials in this regard.

Here, attempt has been made to describe the study of two French scholars, namely A.M. Hocart and Louis Dumont. A.M. Hocart in his book *Caste: A Contemporary Study* (1950) presented a comparative account of different castes involved in caste system. He described that each caste maintained its identity through prohibition on food and marriage. But this could not be meant that each caste was in isolation. They were interrelated, interdependent and maintained coexistence. Functional dependency existed among them.

Another French scholar Louis Dumont in his book, *Homo Hierarchicus: An Essay on Caste System* (1970) threw light on homo hierarchicus prevalent in Indian caste system. According to him, caste system united different castes socially and economically. Castes involved in caste system maintained their own identity through observing marriage and food taboos. But they followed the same religion Hinduism. Following the same religion, they were interdependent and interrelated. In other words, different castes maintained structural functional unity through same religion. Thus, castes follow homo hierarchichus.

Characteristics of Caste and Caste System

On the basis of review of different studies conducted on castes and caste system in India, the following characteristics can be noted:

- Caste is a hereditary concept based on birth. Each individual attains his/her caste status on the basis of birth in a particular caste.
- Caste system is a fact for Indian villages in all parts of India.
- In caste system, the position of each caste is fixed. As a result of which stratification is found in caste system such as higher castes, middle castes and lower castes.

- The concept of pollution and purity is found in caste system.
- Brahmin, Kshatriya and Vaishya castes are called twice-born and are entitled for holding *Janeu* (scared thread).
- Some castes occupy the position of dominant caste on the basis of landownership, numerical strength, position in caste hierarchy and religious status.
- In caste system, agricultural castes, artisans and functional castes are interrelated socially and economically through *Jajmani* system.
- Artisan and service castes get payment in kind twice in a year and clothes, grains and money for serving on the occasion of festive and ceremonies, under *Jajmani* system.
- Castes are homo hierarchicus.
- Democratic institutions, education and modern occupation have weakened the caste system.
- Christian and Muslim castes are also involved in *Jajmani* system.
- In caste system social processes like cooperation, competition and conflict are present.
- After independence caste mobility has become a fact.
- Brahmin priest have their *Jajmani* ka village. They can sell or mortgage their *Jajmani* ka village in the hands of another priest.
- Caste based factions and feuds appear in village.
- Changes in caste system have occurred due to social-cultural change processes like Sanskritisation, Westernisation, modernisation, secularisation and democratisation.
- The process of desanskritisation has affected high castes.
- Divinal theory has been propounded for the origin of caste.
- Hereditary, occupational, functional theories for the origin of castes have also been propounded.
- In villages, people use kinship terms to call villagers belonging to any castes.
- Castes have vertical and horizontal solidarity.

5
Urban and Industrial Studies in India

Introduction

In the history of mankind urbanisation is an old process. The prehistoric researches have established the origin of urban centres as early as 5000 years ago. The prehistoric urban centres of Mohen Jodaro, Harappa, Chanhudaro, Lothal were followed by ancient cities of Kasi, Prayag, Mathura, Ayodhya, Gaya, Patliputra, Rajgir, Prayagraj, Haridwar, Puri and others. They emerged in ancient time either as religious or religio-administrative towns. These towns were greatly integrated with the respective regions and in several cases with the whole of India. These urban centres in Redfieldian terminology were of "Orthogenetic origin" and represented the primary phase of urbanisation in civilizational frame of India.

During Muslim period, specially during the period of Akbar, Shershah and other city builders, towns like Agra, Delhi, Jodhpur, Firozpur, Daulatabad, Fatehpur Sikri, Farrukhabad and several others were established. These were mainly administrative centres dotted with forts, mosques, tombs, and other palatial buildings of several Muslim rulers.

When British came to India with advance technology and scientific knowledge and commercial motivations, the process of urbanisation took a definite turn which marked the beginning of urbanisation based on industrialisation. This phase of urbanisation was characterised by exploitation of mineral resources, establishment of mineral-based industries, investment of foreign capital and employment of foreign technicians. These eventually led to the emergence of mining, industrial, commercial, transportational including port towns and administrative set-up of large magnitude. With these along with the expansion of pre-existing traditional cities of India located on the bank of rivers, confluence of rivers and rivers with sea and their fertile valleys, a number of mining and industrial centres came into existence in hilly and forested areas of India. All these led to secondary process of urbanisation which continued with accelerated speed after Independence in India. In the contemporary time, with the technical aid from several countries, large scale industrialization was possible in many areas of our country. The urban population has increased in different states of India. There has been a considerable growth of urban centres in geographically isolated hilly and forested regions.

In spite of cultural roles of cities in India in the past and industrial role in present, the study of towns and cities in India has been taken up quite recently. In the West, the industrial revolution had taken place long ago, but enquiry into the life of people appeared in 1902 with great and pioneering work of Charles Booth under the title *Life of People of London*. In India first detailed urban survey was conducted by D.R. Gadgil of Gokhale Institute of Politics and Economics in 1936-37. The first volume of report was made available in print in 1945 and second volume of report appeared in 1952. The publication of Gadgil's report marked the beginning of constructive phase of urban study in India.

In the background of efforts made by census operations, Gazetteer writings, British scholars and leadership of Gadgil, a number of geographers, economists, demographers, sociologists and social anthropologists took up the task of urban and industrial studies in India.

Several organisations like Research Programme Committee of Planning Commission, UNESCO Research Centre, various individual university scholars took up study of urban centre and urbanisation in India. A review of all urban and industrial studies made by different scholars on urban and industrial study is being presented here under two broad headings:

- Urban and Industrial study in Pre-Independence Period.
- Urban and Industrial study in Post-Independence Period.

Urban and Industrial study in Pre-Independence Period

The earliest record dealing with urban life in India was by Rev

M.A. Sherring. On the basis of ancient scriptures and his own field investigation, he published his book, *The Sacred City of Hindu: An Account of Banaras in Ancient and Modern Times* (1868). In this book, he described the picture of urban life in Banaras.

J.R. Blackwood in his book *Calcutta Town and Suburb* (1902) presented a sketchy pictures of socio-economic life in Calcutta.

H.T. Sorley published a book *Cities of Bombay Presidency* (1931) and presented a most factual description of cities specially of Bombay.

In addition to these individual publications, the *Imperial Gazetteers of India* was published in 34 volumes in the year 1907 and 1908. In these volumes precise description related to Indian cities were presented in terms of origin, history, population, administration, trade, commerce, industries, famine, medical facility, education and others. A set of 105 cities were described under these 34 volumes of *Imperial Gazetteers of India*. They provided baseline data of those 105 urban centres.

Besides Imperial Gazetteers, the *District Gazetteers of India*—original and revised ones—gave us some basic informations on cities and towns of India. The Census Operation of India since its inception continued to collect data on population, occupation, religion, language, literacy and towns and cities of various sizes. In spite of several limitations of census data, the volumes of census provided the base line data as well as comparable materials from towns of different parts of India. They were and are useful in understanding the process of urbanisation in India.

Urban and Industrial Study in the Post-independence Period

After Independence of India, the problem of urbanisation and industrialisation was recognised by the Government. The need was felt for field investigation and analytical enquiry for preparation of five years plan to provide solutions to the problems. The Research Programme Committee was set up by Planning Commission in July 1952 to finance and encourage survey of various kinds. In less than a period of 4 years, 21 cities and towns were surveyed with emphasis on rural-urban migration and employment opportunities associated with rapid urbanisation. The main objective behind the survey of 21 cities and towns were as follows:

- To study features of urbanisation such as commercial and industrial establishments and increase in population.
- To explore employment opportunities provided by organised, unorganised and commercial sectors.
- To highlight nature and extent of migration.
- To delineate urban employment.
- To describe problem of urbanisation like housing, drinking water, road, electricity, transport, health and social amenities.

Due to financial support from Planning Commission, universities and research institutions were involved in survey work of cities in India. Although lion's share of financial support went to economists, few geographers, sociologists and anthropologists also received financial assistance to undertake study of cities in India organised by Planning Commission.

In 1952, UNESCO sponsored a special comparative study of urbanisation in several South Asian countries. With its headquarters at Calcutta, UNESCO Research Centre on Social Implication of Industrialisation in South Asia, made several impressive studies of towns like Bangkok, Bombay, Dacca, Delhi, Djakarta, and established an emerging steel city of India. With rich resources, UNESCO produced not only several excellent works on urban studies, but also encouraged several researches of universities and research institutions to take up study of urbanisation in their respective regions on an interdisciplinary level.

Under the influence of Chicago School of Social Anthropology, the need was felt to study the cultural roles of cities and their contributions in the development of India's civilization. Such an anthropological approach to study Indian civilization in terms of various dimensions, folk, peasant and urban, attracted researchers in the study of complex society in India. Among the important researches conducted in this line were Milton Singer's study on Madras City, Vidyarthi's on Gaya City, Marriott's on Wai town, and Oraon's on Jameshedpur. All these city studies not only provided fresh materials but also encouraged several researchers to take up study of Rajgir, Deoghar, Janakpur, Varanasi, Prayag, Ayodhya, Mathura, Dwarka, Somnath, Badrinath, Kedarnath, Haridwar, Tirupati, Rameshwaram, Nasik and others.

Indian Sociological Association, Bombay and Economic

Association introduced the topic of industrialization in their annual meetings. With increasing interest in urbanisation studies, different seminars were organised by different universities including California (1960) and Ranchi (1961). In these seminars, problems of urbanisation and industrialisation were discussed and attempt was made to know social-cultural change in India.

Work of Urban Geographers

Geographers, whose primary aim has been to study man in relation to his environment, showed interest in the study of growth, distribution, size, and function of cities. A number of full-length study were made by geographers.

R.L. Singh in his book *Banaras: A Study in Urban Geography* (1955) and *Mirzapur: A Study in Urban Geography* (1960) described the relation between man and environment of Banaras and Mirzapur.

D. Majumdar in his book *Urban Pattern of Siliguri* (1957) presented the urban pattern of Siliguri town.

A.R. Tiwari in his research paper, "Urban Regions of Agra" (1958) described the urban areas of Agra town.

A.B. Chatterjee in his research paper, "Demographic Features of Howrah City" (1958) described the demographic features of Howrah city. He described sex ratio and density of population.

A.K. Dutta in his research paper, "The Neighbourhood Unit Plan and its Impact on Jamshedpur" (1962) presented the urban pattern of Jamshedpur town.

Ujagar Singh in his research paper, "KAVAL" (1966) explored the geographical features of Kanpur, Allahabad, Varanasi, Agra and Lucknow and made a comparison between them.

N.K. Kar of Calcutta University conducted a research project on "The Problem of Regional Planning of Lower West Bengal", (1962).

Enayat Ahmad in his research paper, "Size and Function of Towns and Cities of India" (1958), brought out brilliantly geographical factors in the development of size and function of towns and cities of Uttar Pradesh and Bihar. He discovered the concentration of town in Bihar in triangle where Ganges left Bihar and Gandak and Sone entered the state. This triangle had been the cultural heart of Bihar since time immemorial and presently included the region of sugar, cement, and tobacco industries leading to the highest density of rural population in the state. He established that half of towns of state were located within one-third of total area formed by the triangle. He divided the state of Bihar into seven umblands of cities, namely Muzaffarpur, Darbhanga, Bhagalpur, Patna, Gaya, Ranchi and Jamshedpur. Among these cities of Bihar and Jamshedpur represented the extreme type of urbanisation.

In most of these studies regional urbanisation study was done and study of urbanisation of an individual town in detail was lacking.

Study of Economists

Economists conducted most of urban studies sponsored by Planning Commission. With the financial support of Research Programme Committee, the city of Poona was restudied by N.V. Sovani and others (1956) of Gokhale Institute of Politics and Economics. The report was published as *Poona: A Resurvey* (1956). Data were gathered in 1954 and compared to the earlier study of Poona by D.R. Gadgil (1952). In the restudy of Poona, 4 per cent households were surveyed.

The next socio-economic survey of Hyderabad-city Secundarabad city was undertaken by another economist Keshava Iyengar and was published under the title *A Socio-economic Survey of Hyderabad Secunderabad city area* (1957). 2.68 per cent households of the total were sampled for study. The survey was conducted for one year from July 1954. In the general framework set by Research Programme Committee, the survey covered population, migration, industry, earning, income, employment, housing condition and social life. The survey also covered fertility and family planning on the basis of 493 cases of women. The survey failed to cover the rural background of migrants, caste, class and religion.

The socio-economic survey of Baroda city was undertaken by Malkani and published under the title, *A Socio-economic Survey of Baroda City* (1955). The period covered under survey was July 1954 to March 1955. 10 per cent out of 4202 households were selected randomly. Attempts were made to find out extent of migration in the city since 1941 and the nature of unemployment prevalent in various sections of population. The report was full of statistical tables, but social variables like caste, religion, language were not covered.

The socio-economic survey of Jamshedpur city was conducted by B.R. Mishra (1959). His survey included economic variables like population, commercial and industrial establishments, employment, nature of migration, unemployment and problems of housing, transport, power, water supply and social amenities. He had selected 5 per cent samples on stratified sampling basis. But study totally ignored social variables.

The socio-economic survey of Surat was conducted and report was submitted in 1957 by N.B. Desai. The period of survey was July 1954 to October 1954. He also conducted survey on Gorakhpur in the same period. He emphasized on fertility rate and family planning in the survey of both cities.

The socio-economic survey of Hubali was undertaken by Dhekney (1959). The survey was made for six months in 1954. He confined his study on migration, occupation, employment, income, living standards, housing condition, incidence of urban employment. For the purpose of study, 11 per cent samples were drawn randomly. Besides economic variables, he had included social variables like mother tongue, literacy, size and structure of family. The rural background of migrants and their respective links with native places were also covered. Like Poona restudy Dhekney was able to find out poverty line. 85.5 per cent of families were found below the poverty line of Rs. 450 per anum per adult unit. On the basis of survey, he suggested for the development of indigenous industrial and commercial enterprises and to overcome the lack of resourcelessness. He brought out more sociological data than other economists who had made survey of cities.

The socio-economic survey of Calcutta was undertaken by S.N. Sen (1961). The socio-economic survey of metropolitan Calcutta city was conducted from early 1954 to early 1959 for five years. The study was based on selected households. Those living in army barracks, jails, hospitals and individuals without fixed residence were excluded from the survey. The study highlighted occupation, income, migration, displaced migrants and population growth in the city. The study pointed out problems like food requirement, influx of job seekers, more employment opportunity, more investment in housing, investment in slum clearance, transports, schools, colleges, hospitals and social amenities. He suggested for a total provision of at least Rs. 300-350 crore in five years for development of Calcutta metropolitan city. The author brought out the fact that like Kanpur, the metropolitan population of Calcutta was too masculine (63% male and 35% female). Considering this he pleaded for restriction on movement of migrants in the city.

The socio-economic survey of cosmopolitan city Bombay was conducted by D.T. Lakdawala (1962). The survey was conducted from August 1954 to March 1955 and included 13,369 households (2.7% of total households). On the pattern of Calcutta, the survey excluded street-dwellers, hutment dwellers and hostilities. He emphasised upon economic variables such as occupation, income, migration, employment, population and social amenities.

P.C. Malhotra made a socio-economic survey of Bhopal city (1964). He made survey about occupation, income, family composition, housing condition, besides problem of migration, employment and unemployment.

V.K.R.V. Rao and P.B. Desai made socio-economic survey of greater Delhi and came to the conclusion that due to Second World War, the city of Delhi witnessed large scale migration and had to face a number of problems in accommodating migrants into its economy.

D.S. Chauhan made socio-economic study of Agra (1965) and highlighted the problem of adaptation process of migrants in Agra city.

Study of Anthropologists and Sociologists

The Research Programme Committee of Planning Commission, Government of India, had assigned the task of urban studies to sociologists to explore sociological problems of urban-dwellers and suggest for solving those problems. Sociologists working in Institutes of Social Work were involved in it.

The study of Beggar problem of Madras city was done by K.N. George (1956). The fieldwork was conducted for eight months by four sociologists under the directorship of K.N. George. The report running into 71 pages with 34 statistical tables dealt with nature of beggar problem, phases in growth of beggary and ended with recommendations.

An another similar survey of beggar problem in metropolitan Delhi was sponsored by Planning Commission in Delhi. The study was conducted by M.S. Gore of Delhi School of Social Work (1956). The survey work was carried out by a team of a dozen investigators for the period of ten months in 1954-55. The report presented a detailed account of nature of beggars, problems, types of beggars, their community life and suggested measures for tackling the problem of beggar.

According to analysis of data, male beggars were more in number than female beggars in both cities—Madras and Delhi. A bulk of them were able-bodied and enjoyed normal health. The causes of beggary were poverty, beggary profession of a family, harsh treatment of parents, loss of parents in early age and unguided childhood. The areas of operation and technique of begging of Delhi beggars were somewhat different from Madras beggars. Delhi baggers were not found in state of social isolation. They lived with families and friends. The community alignment was based on two considerations—common language and common disease leprosy. The Delhi Survey appeared to be more informative and of higher standard than Madras survey. These surveys were pilot project carried out to test the methods and tools of survey, but they lacked multifaceted social and cultural problem of beggars. The Delhi study suggested that begging as pattern of behaviour could not be understood only as a process of interaction between baggers and givers. George examined the problem of begging in historical perspective and suggested gradual transition from repressive to preventive and then to rehabilitative measures. M.S. Gore was assigned an another problematic research project by Research Programme Committee for child welfare services and institutions in Delhi.

Mrs. P. Sengupta undertook a pilot survey to study the scope for employment of women in Jute Industry, Titagarh (1960) sanctioned by Research Programme Committee. The survey was completed in six months (November 1956 to March 1957). The project aimed to suggest new avenues for employment of women labourers who had lost jobs since 1957 due to rationalisation in Jute factory and framing of new industrial laws related to women employment. The report brought out a fact that unemployment and underemployment of women was not a problem in Jute industry alone, but it was typical of bigger industry. The report suggested for the distribution of lands through Bhoodan movement for landless immigrants and boosting up of the village and cottage industries.

S.D. Punekar and Miss Kamala Rao made study of prostitutes of Bombay financed by Research Programme Committee under the auspices of Association for Moral and Social Hygiene, Maharashtra Branch. The report was published in the form of book *A Study of Prostitutes in Bombay* (1962).

Altogether 44 per cent women (370 prostitutes and 74 mistress) and life histories of 425 women out of 5,000 prostitutes were covered under the study. Data were gathered by a team of researchers from prostitutes living in "tolerated areas" of Bombay city. Within tolerated areas, the existence of prostitutes was tolerated by general public, local authorities and police. The project aimed to study emotional, social, and economic aspects of early life of respondents, various aspects of their marital life, their mode of living during separation period from husband and family and causes of taking up prostitution. The study also attempted to know social, economic, physical conditions of their life in prostitution, their leisure time activity, attitudes towards their profession and future life. Punekar studied in detail about various aspects and problems of prostitutes. He classified prostitutes into two categories: *Deodasis* and Non-*deodasis*. No single cause appeared regarding leading a life as prostitute. He recorded 26 factors responsible for entering into this trade, the major being emotional, economic, social, physical and physiological. Majority of prostitutes had unsatisfactory childhood. They viewed their profession as unemotional and detached manner as a source of their livelihood. Illiteracy was prevalent in 90 per cent prostitutes. The data did not support poverty as an important cause of prostitution. He recommended for the removal of tolerated areas from the city and rehabilitation of prostitutes through vocational training and guidelines. He also suggested to make study of men involved in prostitution as customers, procurers and pimps for the full understanding of the problem.

R.K. Mukherjee and Baljit Singh studied Lucknow city financed by Research Programme Committee and published their book under the title *Social Problems of a Metropolis* (1961). The survey work of this city was conducted during April 1954 to June 1955. 15 per cent of households were sampled on the basis of stratified random sampling. The fieldwork was conducted by team of researchers consisting of sociologists and economists. Thus, inter-disciplinary approach was adopted in the study of Lucknow city. The book was divided into two parts. The chapters included in first part were 10 in number dealing with civil amenities, trends in urbanisation, factors of migration, employment in organised and unorganised sectors, unemployment and housing condition. Chapters included in Part II were on fertility pattern and family planning. The study claimed to emphasise the sociological aspect of city life and analysis of caste and family system was made. Joint family system was found living outside the city. The lack of old age and sickness assurances appeared as an obstacle in permanent settlement in towns of all immigrant households. The report presented poor living standards, general poverty, inadequacy of public utilities and civic amenities.

The study of Kanpur city was undertaken by D.N. Majumdar under the sponsorship of Research Programme Committee with a view to explore complex conditions of urban life in an industrial metropolis. Based on this study, Majumdar published his book *Social Contours of an Industrial city—Social Survey of Kanpur* (1960). On the basis of his enquiry as a social anthropologist, Majumdar made a departure from the routine type of socio-economic survey of a city. He initiated a major probe into the city factory life. A schedule was prepared to study social and cultural factors which were characterising, distinguishing, assisting and impeding the qualitative changes in the work of industrialisation. Despite his interest in socio-cultural implication of industrialisation and applying schedule over 2000 people, Majumdar had to limit his study in the line of similar studies conducted by RPC of Planning Commission. The book was divided into three parts. Each part had a number of chapters. The book described general features, survey and family planning enquiry. The book ended with an independent section on cultural content of urbanisation.

In the first part of the book, growth of Kanpur as an industrial metropolis through decades, present day civic amenities, nature and extent of industrial employment and unemployment were discussed. The report brought out as to how number of factories increased in the beginning of 20th century and the streets of Kanpur came to have electric lights in 1909. Employment increased in the city and a regular census was taken in 1906. Reviewing the present day civic problems, the author found city full of slums, insanitation, poor public health, absence of planned shopping centres. He highlighted absence of civic amenities in several villages like settlements on the fringe of the city particularly on the southern bordering of Kanpur. There were 273 factories in 1953 providing employment to 68,832 workers. He referred to growing unemployment among educated youngmen and suggested several types of vocational and training and effective service of employment exchange.

In second section, Majumdar presented field data collected on the basis of sample survey and analysed both migrants and non-migrants as a masculine city. He observed that 43.85 per cent immigrants came to the city due to pull factors. He classified the people of Kanpur engaged in 63 occupations which were further divided into 29 categories.

The report of family planning and fertility envisaged a coverage of 5 per cent of city's population among married women. The material was collected from 1525 women by trained sociologists who worked for a period of 5 months from March to July 1955. This portion of report was factual and ran into series of tables on child birth indices, maternity pattern, mortality and survival, birth of twins, attitude towards family planning, mother's view on family size and attitude towards use of contraceptives.

The study gave a statistical data on marriage pattern, husband-wife relationship, attitude of husbands towards status of women and few casual comments regarding caste clustering, social life of migrants and impact of Kanpur on neighbouring villages. It was noted that lower castes from villages found an escape in the city from old stigma of untouchability, while upper castes had lost their importance in religious and institutional fields. He observed that Kanpur could not change the face of villages even adjacent to it except the educated persons of the village were foci of new urban values. Majumdar closed this chapter with following advice:

> "Our towns and cities are growing, our vigilance must not wane, sociologists must line up for social research and help the administration in its assigned task of building an urban population, socially aware and mentally conditioned for city life."

V.S. D'Souza, Head, Department of Sociology, Panjab University, Chandigarh, made study of social structure of a planned city Chandigarh in the light of sociological concepts. His book based on this study was published under the title *Social Structure of a Planned City Chandigarh* (1965). His main emphasis was to study Chandigarh as a community having social structure. According to him, Chandigarh was a newly emerged city settled in planned way, therefore, it was too early to expect stable and coherent social structure. It was inhabited by people coming from different parts of Punjab and other states of India. Being a planned city, the natural process of community organisation was affected by controls inherent in planning.

The study was conducted by applying a schedule on 10 per cent households. The bases of social organisation, occupational structure, educational opportunities, spatial structure, housing and sector as a neighbourhood unit were meaningfully discussed. There were interesting chapters on integration, migration, slum-dwellers and planning Chandigarh as an Indian town. D'Souza brought out a number of indicators to show that community life in Chandigarh was not sufficiently integrated. Both at the level of city and sector, there were no signs of organised community life. There was no recognised leadership either in religious, cultural or political realm of life at the level of sector and city. The participation in social life in terms of membership of voluntary associations or other community activities was meagre. 70 per cent people continued ties with home community—wife and children, other close relatives and immovable properties and consequently frequent visits. This acted as a check on feeling of belonging together in community.

D'Souza considered it as a superimposed city on a distinct Indian cultural landscape. The sector theory of American neighbourhoods which comprised cluster of families belonging to a single social stratum with school, hospital, recreational centres did not fit in Indian situation. The study indicated that differences in social levels in different sectors were developing certain cleavages between different classes. This was noticeable in employment opportunities for children. Such trends were against social and political goals of democracy and socialism. D'Souza suggested that in order to achieve different goals of cohesiveness, progressiveness, democracy and socialism, it was necessary to have mixed neighbourhood in which social differences were articulated skilfully to hide glaring inequality and where there was opportunity for people of different classes to interact.

L.P. Vidyarthi in his book *Cultural Configuration of Ranchi* (1969) had attempted to highlight the cultural patterns of Ranchi city. He had attempted to know origin, history, form and function of Ranchi city empirically. He had tried to show interaction between tribal and peasant villages to Ranchi city and relation between tribal and non-tribal in the context of Ranchi city. According to him increase in population of Ranchi city occurred due to establishment of administrative offices, Railway stations, commercial and trade related institutions and educational institutions in and around Ranchi. Vidyarthi wanted to highlight the role of Ranchi city as a regional centre. Because the city of Ranchi had brought changes in life and culture of tribal villages situated nearby it. He wanted to establish Ranchi as a tribal city. He presented a monographic study of Ranchi town. He attempted to know historical, geographical, demographic, social, cultural, economic, religious, political and administrative characteristics of Ranchi town.

The study of Ranchi city was financed by Research Programme Committee, Planning Commission, Government of India. In order to study the city of Ranchi, entire research project was divided into three phases: (i) Pilot survey, (ii) Fieldwork, (iii) Data processing and report writing. Besides questionnaire and schedule techniques, participant and non-participant observation, interview, genealogical table, case study and life history techniques of data collection were employed. For pilot study two months, for fieldwork 10 months and for data processing and report writing 4 months were determined. But data processing and report writing took more time. The main objective behind the study of Ranchi city were as follows:

- To provide intimate data in supplementing the findings arrived at by sampling survey methodology.
- To understand affairs of tribal and non-tribal groups living in and around Ranchi.
- To study the influence of Ranchi on its expanding hinterlands.
- To delineate processes and direction of change in tribal culture in urban, sub-urban and rural setting.

- To test, refine and reformulate hypothesis of rural-urban continuum developed by Robert Redfield.

Applying questionnaires and schedule on 10 per cent samples, anthropological survey of four localities, urban institutions and selected villages as well as information gathered from secondary sources, Vidyarthi described the cultural configuration of Ranchi city in holistic manner. The study appeared to be more analytical and interpretative than statistical and descriptive.

Among the other sociological and social anthropological studies of urbanisation were sponsored by UNESCO Research Centre in 1953-55. The project covered researches on Bangkok by Robert B. Textor, on Bombay by P.N. Prabhu, on Dacca by A.R.A. Hussain, on Djakarta by Institute of Economic and Social Research and Delhi by M.D. Deshmukh. The result of these researches were published under the title, *The Social Implication of Industrialisation and Urbanisation* (1956).

The study of Bombay by Prabhu was based on a sample of 23 households selected to explore the general idea about socio-economic conditions and cultural life of people of Bombay city. The study reflected that nearly all migrants came to the city and took service out of despair because they had no alternative. They expressed their discontentment with city life and wished to settle in villages after retirement. The caste system was not rigidly followed. Class based discrimination and differentiation appeared. The report gave us information about socio-psychological adjustment of migrants. The city-dwellers observed punctuality, precision, accuracy and uniformity in formal roles and rules. They faced physical and psychological strains in making journey to and from place of work. Media of commercialised recreation like cinema appeared in their life. Smoking, drinking, gambling, tea taking and visiting the prostitutes had influenced the life of city-dwellers. The religious faith was undergoing gradual change due to modern material and cultural forces.

The study of Deshmukh on aimless floating migrants in Delhi was of special significance. The floating migrants were defined as persons who left their village after 1939 in urban areas in search of employment and since then were floating from town to village. The study was mainly concerned with migrants from Marathi speaking Madhya Pradesh comprising ten districts.

The study was completed in three rounds. In first round, the condition of 41 villages of regions of Madhya Pradesh were studied during September 1950 and 1953. In the second, round study of movements of some migrant families was made with a view to find out routine forwarded by them in month of April, May and June 1953. In the third round, study of conditions under which migrants lived and worked was made in 8 towns. The family budget survey work in Delhi was completed in one year in between August 1953 to July 1954.

In course of survey attempt was made to explore and describe on employment, income, expenditure, consumption, health, beggary, delinquency, prostitution, family disorganisation and breakdown of family customs. It was found that good number of migrant families did not like vagabond life and wanted to settle down somewhere permanently. Migration has led to personal and social disorganisation. It was observed that a typical migrant became a marginal man in whom traits of rural and urban was very active who was a sufferer from a cultural shocks. The researcher discussed about various types of migrants and their stages. The extent of marginality was reflected in different types of migrants.

In the next stage of urban studies undertaken by UNESCO Research Centre covered all steel cities of India such as Jamshedpur, Burhanpur, Bhadravati, Rourkela, Bhilai and Durgapur. The study started in September 1958 aimed at collecting data on growth of steel town scattered in various reports and journals, pointing out major gaps in material collected and analysing major problems of urbanisation in steel towns. The study provided readers with understanding of urbanism as a way of life and urbanisation as a process of transforming the ways of life.

The UNESCO report on steel city of Jamshedpur was available in library of Tata Iron and Steel Company. The report provided material about physical, demographic, economic, social, cultural and personal accounts of Jamshedpur Steel City. The earlier studies on Jamshedpur were done by following scholars:

- Verrier Elwin: *The Story of Tata Steel*, Bombay, 1958.
- B.R. Mishra: *Report on Socio-economic Survey Jamshedpur*, 1959.
- A.K. Dutta: *The Neighbourhood Unit Plan and its Impact on Jamshedpur*, 1962.

- P.G. Ganguli: *Growth of Jamshedpur and Some Aspects of Tribal Change*, 1958.

The preliminary report of UNESCO Research Centre on Growth of Steel Towns in India (1960) presented a model of urban study and took into account economic, demographic, social, cultural and psychological variables in the analysis of urbanisation. Under economic implications characteristics of traditional economy—folk and peasant—found around the city were discussed. The social implications were understood as under social differentiation, solidarity, social stratification, social administrator, administration, and social welfare. It found community uprooted from rural context in the state of disintegration. The grouping was based on sex, age, political views, parent state and dialects. A potential unskilled tribal labour commuting between neighbouring villages and towns were responsible for carrying urban influence far beyond its municipal limits. The report also discussed a number of active and dormant tribal organisations. It found tribal community welding itself into reemergent force. Although the joint family was disintegrating, but family was indicating rural-urban continuum. The family was found to be preservative of caste system in house, but not in factory and towns. It also reflected fundamental differential in 1st, 2nd, 3rd generations. There were two classes—managerial class and working class. The city administration was in the control of company and the philosophy of paternalism was guiding principle of city administration. The practice of paternalism led to the lack of civic consciousness dulled public initiative, creeping up of an idea that individuals were employees and never citizens and it prevented the healthy trade unionism. Under social welfare housing, electricity, water supply, sewage system, dairy farm, public health, hospitals, education and community welfare. *Bastee* welfare and tribal welfare were studied carefully. In the matters of housing accommodation and educational facility distinction was made between tribals and non-tribals and between employees and non-employees. Tribals were forced to feel as if they were orphaned. The emergence of pan-tribalistic ideology is manifested in three forces of revivalism, selective detribalisation and selective modernisation. In dialectical parlance detribalisation was thesis, revivalism the antithesis and pan-tribalism the synthesis.

The study of Jamshedpur was also unique in the sense that it indicated lines on which studies could be undertaken to assist the growth of human personality under the impact of large scale industry and a rapidly growing town. It suggested that in the light of concept of basic personality structure, the characteristics of 'steel man' might be analysed. The nature of crime and related deviant behaviour in industrial city needed to be studied. On the whole, UNESCO study of Jamshedpur was one of the most authentic, wisely analysed and systematically conceived on social implications of industrialisation in a steel city of India.

The study of industrial urbanism in folk and tribal areas of middle India had attracted the attention of L.P. Vidyarthi, a leading social anthropologist and Head, Department of Anthropology, Ranchi University, Ranchi to study the Socio-cultural Implications of Industrialization in tribal areas of the then Bihar and now Jharkhand state. He in his book *Socio-cultural Implications of Industrialisation: A Case Study of Tribal Bihar* (1970), attempted to discuss the socio-cultural implications of industrialisation in tribal area of Chotanagpur. The book provided an excellent case study for understanding form and process of cultural change caused by emergence of factories in an underdeveloped area. The study of Hatia industrial complex provided a case for longitudinal analysis of various phases of industrialisation. The author tried to understand the socio-cultural implications of industrialisation through three phases.

- Formulatory phase
- Constructive phase
- Productive and elaborative phase.

Formulatory Phase

The formulatory phase induced the uprooting of folk and peasant society and its problem of rehabiliation.

Constructive Phase

This phase include the installation of factory, township and commercial network.

Productive and Elaborative Phase

This phase included full-fledged production and industrial style of living.

The fieldwork was started in 1958 in villages like Hatia, Latma and Satranji. They were to be removed completely in first spell of industrialisation. A full length ethnographic study of these villages was made and initial reactions of villagers towards an industrial complex were recorded. When villages were acquired, and problem of rehabilitation arose, various situations were studied. A number of research investigators were employed to collect data on changes introduced by industrial activities. It was felt that the problem of adjustment was more acute in the initial phase of industrial establishment and less when factory started work.

Taking spatial expansion of industrial complex and its radiating influence, it was noted that with the passage of time industrial core also underwent geographical expansion. At second stage, three concentric regions of expansion and influence appeared. They are as follows:

- The core of industrial complex
- The fringe of industrial complex
- The margin of industrial complex.

The first circle with a radius of five miles covered all factories, township, dam, railway station, official building, 8 uprooted villages and also the village Hatia which is standing in the core of industrial complex.

The second concentric circle extended beyond the first circle but up to a radius of 10 miles from the industrial core and included 150 villages. The village located within the fringe of industrial centre were thoroughly studied selecting four villages of different circles and different nature. Here attempt was made to have a comparative look on their demography, economy and socio-religious customs of pre- and post-industrial period.

The third concentric circle extended up to 20 miles from industrial core covered more than 200 villages and constituted the industrial marginal circle. This belt seemed to be less affected by industrial core. Its impact was recorded in 4 villages located at different distances within the margin of industrial complex.

These three circles—core, fringe and margin of industrial complex were studied in their formulatory, constructive, productive and elaborative phases.

This book of Vidyarthi was divided into three parts. The part first consisted of three chapters in which description of societies of pre-industrial and Hatia industrial complex was presented. This part dealt with those tribal and peasant villages which were uprooted for establishment of Hatia industrial complex. Here description of formulatory and constructive phases of industrialisation was presented. Industrial relation and labour union movement also found presentation in this part.

The part second consisted of six chapters. Here, description of societies of factory workers and slum-dwellers was made. Their income, expenditure, occupation, mobility, migration and status of working was made in detail.

The part third of the book consisted of seven chapters in which impact of urbanisation on different kinds of selected villages was dealt with. Description of nature of social, economic, political and psychological changes was discussed elaborately. New style of life under the influence of urbanisation and problem of unemployment were highlighted.

Thus, Vidyarthi formulated and tested a number of concepts related to industrial urbanisation and dealt the process and impact of urbanisation in tribal belt of Chotanagpur in this book. This book is significant contribution to urban and industrial anthropology.

B.R. Chauhan, in his Book *Town in Tribal Setting* (1970) described the process and impact of industrialisation on tribal life. Chauhan had chosen tribal district of Banswara in Rajasthan where 70 per cent population was of Scheduled Tribes. A sample of 377 households was drawn from two towns and four villages. The focus of study was on process of diffusion of urban elements in tribal villages. On the basis of comparative study of rural and urban institutions, Chauhan established the nature of rural-urban interaction.

G.S. Aurora in his book, *Tribe Caste Class Encounter: Aspects of Folk-urban Relation in Alirajpur Tehsil* (1972) examined some aspects of folk-urban relation in the context of Alirajpur Tehsil, an administrative sub-division of Jhabua district in Madhya Pradesh. He did field research in tribal village of Bamanta and town of

Alirajpur. The book made an interesting effort in understanding tribe, caste and class. He suggested that Sanskritisation came in this region with political intrusion of Rajput caste dynasties. The marketing centre provided the linkage between kinship relations at regional level. The process of diffusion from the marketing centre to the peripheries and from towns to tribal villages indicated the universalisation and modernisation and secularisation. Aurora noted that in this sub-region there were tribes which might be termed as rural castes and urban castes with weaker tribal consciousness.

Another trend of urban study in India was related to folk-urban continuum which examined the effect of urbanisation on traditional culture. Related to this was interest in study of traditional city as dimension of Indian civilisation. American anthropologist Robert Redfield propounded the concept of folk-urban continuum and great tradition and little tradition to understand the interaction between folk and urban communities. He did not consider folk and urban community in isolation, rather interrelated and interdependent and maintaining interaction. Little community like folk and peasant had little tradition characterised by illiteracy, magic and simple structure and great community like towns, cities and metropolises had great traditions characterised by religions, literacy and complex structure. Little tradition and great tradition were ideal type polar opposite concept. They originated at two different places—folk and urban, but not in isolation. They were interrelated, interdependent and complementary to each other.

Robert Redfield and Milton Singer in their research paper, "Cultural Role of City" (1956), discussed in detail the cultural role of a city. After publication of this paper, Indian anthropologists started studying the cultural role of city. Each city had a town deity as cultural centre, where cultural performances were done with the help of cultural specialists. Each culture centre had cultural media like *Bhajan, Kirtan,* song and published booklet. These cultural centres acted as media of culture transmission and attracted not only town-dwellers but also village-dwellers at regional and national level. Thus, city plays significant cultural role.

Milton Singer in his paper, "Great Tradition in Metropolitan Centre of Madras", (1958) noted three methods of localising the great tradition in limited area. They were as follows:

- Through the study of sacred geography.
- Through the study of professional representatives and their social organisation.
- Through cultural performances including religious rites and ceremonies.

In this study, Singer presented the sacred geography and the social organisation of Madras city. He presented a historical account of cultural performances along with regional extension.

Keeping concepts propounded by Robert Redfield and Milton Singer in the study of cultural roles of city, Vidyarthi made study of a traditional city Gaya and published his book, *Sacred Complex of Hindu Gaya* (1961). This study was related to Hindu Civilisation. Vidyarthi developed three concepts to test in this study. They were: sacred geography, sacred specialist and sacred performance. These three concepts together constituted sacred complex. He attempted to test concepts propounded by Redfield and Singer in a new context. He had formulated and tested following hypotheses in studying sacred complex of Hindu Gaya:

- Sacred complex is a happy synthesis of sacred geography, sacred specialist and sacred performance.
- A Hindu pilgrimage centre shows continuum organisation and compromise between great tradition and little tradition.
- The sacred specialist of a place with their distinctive style of life transmit certain elements of great tradition to the rural population of India.
- The sacred complex has been in the process of modification and transformation.

Vidyarthi was very clear in his stand with certain necessary specification. He applied the term Hindu Civilisation, not Indian civilization and in place of culture he used the term sacred to evolve the analytical concepts of sacred geography, sacred specialist and sacred performance. He used term sacred complex to integrate pattern envisaging all sacred elements.

The period of field study was 1948 to 1956. The sacred complex of Gaya was predominantly a great tradition. He found out a peculiar process of combination and compromise in the past leading to the development of Hinduism. The sacred complex provided a meeting place of various kinds of people, tradition, caste, sects, class and status and nourished a sense of Indian unity even at a time when spirit of nationalism was lacking. He observed that sacred complex was undergoing secondary urbanisation which remained to be studied in future. Following methodology and approach of Vidyarthi, his students made study of sacred complex of Janakpur, Rajgir, Vaidyanathdham, Kashi, Prayag, Ayodhya, Mathura, Dwarika, Haridwar, Badrinath, Kedarnath, Somnath, Puri, Rameshwaram and Tirupati and published books and papers.

The study of Wai, a shrine town of Maharàshtra was made by McKim Marriott in terms of Redfieldian influences. This paper was unpublished.

Martin Oraon in his research paper on, "Tribal People in an Industrial Setting in India" (1958) presented lifeways of tribals of Jamshedpur Steel city. He described changes occurring in life of Santhal living in industrial city Jamshedpur. He termed Jamshedpur city as ultra modern and less great traditional. He found that Santhals living in *Bustees* nearby Jamshedpur steel city had maintained their separate lifestyle and were not influenced by Hinduism and great tradition.

Cora Du-Bois of Harvard University had studied Bhubaneshwar town (1965). Cora Du-Bois with thirteen American and Indian scholars had studied this sacred town for more than five years but result was not published. The scholars had collected data on following aspects:

- Changes in ritual and administration of Lingraj temple.
- Survey of other temples of Bhubaneshwar.
- Monastic institutions of Bhubaneshwar.
- To study neighbouring villages—Sripur, Naupali, Lakshmisagar and temple village of Kapileshwar.
- Community study of Bhubaneshwar.

The main focus was to study the combination of modernity and tradition in the city of Bhubanseshwar.

K.N. Venkatarayappa made socio-ecological study of Bangalore and published book under the title, *Bangalore: A Socio-economic Study* (1957). He tried to understand social phenomena in ecological context. He had made a comparative study of Bangalore and linked it with region. Following the same methodological pattern, A. Bopemagame studied the city of Delhi and published a book under the title, *Delhi: A Study in Urban Sociology* (1957). The study was based on eight months fieldwork. He had tried to understand the urban pattern of Delhi in the light of sociological theory. Delhi was divided into two halves: old and new. The old Delhi had evolved without any plan, but new Delhi had emerged accidentally according to modern town planning. Material was collected from library and field both. He has attempted to describe history, physical features, population, industry, housing, transport and recreation in his book.

N.K. Bose studied the city of Calcutta and published his book *Calcutta: A Social Survey* (1968). Bose discussed social and cultural life of Calcutta in historical context and brought out the functioning of caste system and other rural traits in metropolitan city of Calcutta. Bose was interested towards the study of Calcutta, when he was Director of Anthropological Survey of India. He planned a socio-cultural survey of Calcutta in June 1962 in collaboration of cultural geographer and a team of other research fellows. The main objectives behind this study were:

- To note distribution of linguistic groups in different parts of metropolis and changes which had taken place.
- To find out similarity and difference in occupations of linguistic groups.
- To study voluntary organisations of different linguistic groups.
- To examine the assessment records of corporation of Calcutta for the years 1911 and 1961.
- To prepare land use maps, nature of houses, roads and the way through which buildings or spaces were used.

On the basis of survey, Bose came to the conclusion that various communities living in Calcutta except Bengalees had more or less built up separate residential concentration of their own. Language also tended to persist. There were schools belonging to Punjabi, Gujarati, Sindhi, Oriya and Hindi speaking people. He found that Bengalee had a strong sense of local patriotism. A Bengali felt happier with company of those with whom he closely agreed, rather than with the company with whom he had differences. Unities were not stressed and differences were not easily tolerated. Calcutta city had witnessed migrants from surrounding districts and from Bihar, Uttar Pradesh and Orissa. Commercial classes came from Delhi, Gujarat and Rajasthan. They had their own caste organisation and they practised it. He observed that Calcutta had developed a kind of rural arrangement which was strongly reminiscent of caste in villages. He referred to caste like segregation in residence and preference to occupation. He suggested that superstructure of cultural pluralism had persisted in civic community of Calcutta and had helped maintaining indirectly communal differences. He further concluded that Calcutta was still in state of immature or imperfect urbanisation. He hoped that with increasing opportunities of employment, the trade unions and professional associations would grow, Calcutta would become more urbanised and freed from narrowness. The book had 85 pages and functional maps of different wards and towns had 210 pages. The cartographic representation covering so many pages seemed to be useful. But it was unfortunate that they had not been referred adequately in the text. The relationship between texts and maps were not properly and clearly indicated.

R.N. Saxena studied refugee of Dehradun and submitted report to Research Programme Committee under the title, *Changing Attitudes and Cultural Assimilation of Refugees Rehabilitated at Dehradun* (1961). He defined refugee as a person who did not like to migrate from homeland, but had to leave due to unbearable and unavoidable conditions—social, political, economic and religious. Out of total 8500 families, 854 were selected randomly for the purpose of study. The study based on interview and questionnaire, recorded the attitude of refugees living in Dehradun towards future life.

I.P. Desai of M.S. University of Baroda, studied the problem of ethical adjustment, economic and religious adjustment in high school of Poona. Data were gathered by questionnaire and interview techniques. The report was submitted to M.S. University of Baroda in 1952.

Desai did an another sociological study of jointness in a small town of Mahua, a seaport on the gulf of Cambay and published book under the title, *Some Aspects of Family in Mahua* (1964). Altogether a sample of 423 households was drawn on the basis of activities of heads of households for earning their livelihood. On the basis of field data, he examined the relation between urbanisation and jointness. He suggested four types of jointness in terms of property and mutual obligations, arranged in ascending and descending order. Those households which were nuclear and did not own property in common with other members outside them, but fulfilled natural obligations—joint family of low degree of jointness.

Those households which were nuclear but owned property with others living in separate households either in Mahua or outside were called as joint family of high degree of jointness.

The households which were so composed that either the addition or subtraction of a member would change the household from joint to nuclear were called marginally joint. They were attributed a high degree of jointness.

The last type of jointness was the traditional type of jointness. Households in which relatives of three or more than three generations live together under a common roof, common hearth, common head and common property were highest degree of jointness. Desai noted that 95 per cent families were showing jointness and 5 per cent families were showing nuclearity. 21 per cent had traditional jointness, 17 per cent had jointness through property, 27 per cent possessed jointness by way of mutual obligation and 30 per cent households were marginally joint. The jointness was more prevalent than anticipated, but jointness was not of traditional type. It was established that longer urban living did not dissolve jointness. Families migrated in Mahua were showing high and low degree of jointness. They were nuclear households with joint ownership of property and mutual obligation with other households. It was observed that the two way processes from nuclearity to jointness and jointness to nuclearity were going on.

A.D. Ross made study of Hindu family in urban setting and published his book under the title *Hindu Family in Urban Setting* (1961). On a highly selective and localised sample Ross attempted to show adjustment pattern of Hindu families in urban surroundings of Bombay. The study highlighted the relational and structural changes in Hindu family.

Jaikar made study of sweepers of Jabalpur city and published his book under the title, *Rural Sweeper in the City* (1952). He attempted to show works performed by sweepers in Jabalpur city and their socio-economic problems. The problem of untouchability at psychological level was highlighted.

P.C. Biswas studied the Shansi, ex-criminal tribe of Delhi and submitted a report to Research Programme Committee (1956). He attempted to highlight historical, social and economic status of Shansi tribes of Delhi, who were termed as ex-criminal tribe.

G.S. Bhat made study of Chamars of Lucknow and published a paper entitled, "Urban Impact and Trends of Intra-caste Solidarity and Dissociability as Measures of Status Mobility among Chamars" (1962). He noted that status mobility in Chamar caste had taken place due to urbanisation. Majority of them had given up traditional occupation and were engaged in other occupations. Some had established shoe repairing centre. Thus, a change in their status had taken place.

An another urban sociologist Hemlata Acharya under the guidance of G.S. Ghurye wrote few papers on urban problems of Nasik. In one of her papers entitled, "An Immigrant Artisan Community" (1955), she studied an artisan caste group of Nasik. She attempted to show physical, cultural and social environment of an Immigrant artisan caste of Nasik. She found that the joint family system of artisan caste was changing in new urban environment of Nasik. The practice of caste occupation was also changing.

In her second research paper entitled, "Urbanising Role of One Lakh City" (1956), she highlighted those factors which were responsible for present day form and size of Nasik town. This town was a pilgrimage centre of Hindus for centuries due to its association with Ram, Sita and Lakshman. It had grown into town of temples in course of time. It was located in rich geographical region. It was commanding a place of modernity in respect to Bombay. These factors led the growth of Nasik in present form.

D.A. Chekki studied Dharwar town of Karnataka and published book under the title *Modernisation and Kinnet Work* (1974). This modern size town had a population of 1,00,000. Based on empirical findings and cross-cultural comparison, the book contributed to the understanding of global problem of modernisation. The book attempted to provide answer of following questions:

- Whether nuclear families were cut-off from kinnetwork.
- Whether nuclear families followed the same pattern in all developing nations.
- Whether transition from pre-urban to urban living necessarily involved stress, strain, conflict and maladjustment.

The foreword of Chekki's book was written by K. Ishwaran, General Editor, Monograph and theoretical study in sociology and anthropology in honour of Nels Anderson. Highlighting the findings, he noted that Chekki's book was a balance between theoretical and monographic study. Chekki had studied the Brahmins of Gokul and Lingayats of Kalyan and described different models of modernisation prevalent in Brahmins and Lingayats.

M.S. Gore studied the process of migration in Bombay and submitted its reports to Tata Institute of Social Sciences under the title, "Immigrants and Neighbourhood: Two Aspects of Life in a Metropolitan City". The research was undertaken under the auspices of Research Programme Committee, but unlike other research project, it provided a depth analysis of process of migration. The study of Gore filled a big gap in our knowledge of rural-urban migration. The report examined various processes of migration and migrant culture. Gore attempted to describe the linguistic pattern of Bombay. There were 45 per cent Marathi, 20 per cent Gujarati, 10 per cent Urdu, 8 per cent Hindi and 17 per cent Tamil, Kannada, Punjabi, Bengali speakers in Bombay. In this sense Bombay appeared to be more heterogeneous than even New York city. In Bombay, English, Hindi, Marathi and Gujarati had co-existence for business, mass communication and education.

K.M. Kapadia and S. Devadas Pillai made study of Atul Bulsar region and published book *Industrialisation and Rural Society* (1972). Atul Bulsar was an industrial town. The book was a valuable addition to the ethnography of industrialising India. The project was initiated by H.M. Kapadia, but conducted and completed by Pillai after his sudden death. The research team worked in the industrial town of Atul Chemical Complex, where one-third of workers lived. The research team also surveyed 12 impact villages from where peasants commuted to factory and five villages without factory workers. Data were gathered by observation, interview, schedule questionnaire techniques. From descriptive account, it appeared that rural people were becoming more conservative regarding women employment and widow remarriage. Peasants wanted factory works not only for high wages, but for convenience of fixed hours, women preferred impersonal employment to domestic service and high castes workers preferred because wages were high.

In addition to the study of specific urban centres and urban problems, few works on general process of urbanisation were published time to time. G.S. Ghurye in second volume of *Sociological Bulletin* published his long articles under the "Cities in India" (1962). In this paper, Ghurye reviewed researches on urban centres and made comment that this number compared with number of similar studies in other countries was by no means sufficient for integrative, economic and cultural needs of a vast country like India. He pointed out towards adaptation of castes due to industrialisation in India. He referred to that freedom from caste restriction on food was seen in city, but they had to follow it in their villages. Thus, people were leading a dual life—separate in villages and separate in city.

Another generalised book on urban culture in India was written by Vidyarthi under the title *Bhartiya Nagar* in Hindi (1966). It was translated in Gujarati by Prof. A. R. Desai and Dr. Meera Desai of Bombay University. This book in seven chapters remade reviews of historical growth of cities in India, classified them from several angles, examined cultural life of urban centres with two case studies—sacred city Gaya and emerging industrial city Ranchi. The book also presented comparative analysis of urban and rural life. The book was based on both literary sources and fieldwork and presented a picture of urbanisation in India.

Ashis Bose in his book *Studies in India's Urbanisation* (1966) had made collection of essays written on urban demography, urban growth, urban planning and urban bibliography.

B.K. Roy Burman studied a small town of Goa named Ponda (1971) and published a booklet dealing with historical, ethnic and demographic features of Ponda—a small Goa town. It also described economic and religious life of town located in heart of an agricultural area. The interaction of Ponda with hinterland in terms of supply of vegetables, milk, fish, coconut, medicine, postal stationery, entertainments and police reflected reciprocal dependency in rural settlement. The importance of Ponda as a place of transmission of modern technology and modern life were shown in the book.

J.S. Tandon in his book *Social Processes in Industrialization of Rourkela,* published by Census Monograph Series (1970) brought to the light demographic, economic and social life of old villages which were uprooted and rehabilitated. The Rourkela Industrial Project was started in 1956 in the original village Rourkela. But it had become a big steel city in a decade with 1,50,000 population covering an area of 30 square miles. 30 villages were uprooted for the establishment of steel complex at Rourkela. The study highlighted process of transmission, disintegration of tribal and peasant style of life and emergence of an industrial society.

Richard C. Fox in his edited volume *Urban India* (1970) had presented social, cultural, educational, economic and anthropological approaches related to urbanisation in India. The book was a collection of ten essays written by several scholars on various themes of urbanisation in India. Essays contributed by scholars were classified into three groups for the purpose of description. They were as follows:

- Urban society
- Urban centre
- Urban form.

Ved Prakash in his book *New Towns in India* (1970) had given a description of 17 new towns situated in 9 states of India. He brought out processes of urban planning, urban development programme and plans of economic development.

R. Trivedi in his book, *Urbanism: A New Outlook* (1976) had presented urbanism in a new outlook. This was an edited book having seven chapters. He in his own paper developed the concept of semi-urban pockets. According to him, semi-urban pockets was third social reality. It had evolved due to imbalance in rural and urban world. He found five types of semi-urban pockets:

- Old army cantonment or police cantonment
- Old and new town
- Refugee colony
- Railway colony
- Industrialized town.

He attempted to throw light on rural-urban continuum through semi-urban pockets.

Bishwa Mohan Mishra in his book *Communication and Modernisation in Urban Slums* (1972) presented a picture of the Delhi slums in context of modernisation, mass communication and urbanisation. Data were gathered from 401 male and female slum-dwellers in Delhi.

Debabrata Banerjee wrote a book, *Personality Characteristics of Unemployed Youth of Calcutta* (1972). The book was revised version of his Ph.D. thesis (1964). The author attempted to understand the ill-effects of unemployment on youth of Calcutta. The study was based on a sample of 200 unemployed youth of Calcutta. Certain psychological conditions of unemployed youth such as neuroticism, self-sufficiency, introversion and being low on dominance and socio-political attitudes towards Government, religion, morality and society were tested to know the personality characteristics of youth of Calcutta.

Satish Sabarwal in his edited book *Beyond Village: Sociological Exploration* (1972) included papers on diverse but specific topics of urban centres such as voting behaviour on a constituency by Atal, sociology of a professional group in small town by Madan, the process of social mobility in Punjabi Urban community by Sabarwal and modernisation of college teachers in Rajasthan by Y. Singh.

Michael M. Ames in his research paper on, "Structural Dimensions of Family Life in Steel City of Jamshedpur" (1975), made a detailed enquiry of structural dimensions of family life in Jamshedpur Steel city. The data were collected in Jamshedpur between September 1967 and June 1968 on management and workers. A survey of 334 Bihari, Bengali and Punjabi workers and supervisors employed by two light engineering firms and residing in company quarters was made for the purpose of study. In the light of survey and in-depth interview, Ames concluded about the structural dimension of family life in Jamshedpur. Workers adapted to pressure of industrialism in flexible and creative ways, and retained certain traditional elements. Workers seemed to operate by two principles—(i) Adjust to the situation for family welfare, and (ii) Limit the adjustment or changes. Family boundaries were made more elastic and familial obligations were made more negotiable, especially within the context of the city. The wider corporate and kinship networks had become supportive institutions. The joint family system facilitated more than obstruction to industrial system. It aided individual mobility at one hand and provided aid and security to its member.

Characteristics of Urban Industrial Society

On the basis of study of urban centres, industrial society and urban civilization by geographers, demographers, economists, administrators, missionaries, sociologists and anthropologists, following characteristics of urban and industrial societies and centres have emerged:

- The builders of Proto-historic Indus Valley Civilization led the foundation of urban centres in our country.
- The builders of Aryan Civilization established a number of great traditional urban centres on banks of rivers or on confluence of rivers and river with sea. They were orthogenetic in origin and showed primary urbanisation.
- Mughal rulers established administrative and capital towns in our country.
- During British period, a number of administrative district towns, capital towns, seaport towns, cantonment towns, mining towns and industrial towns came into existence with heterogenetic origin and they represented secondary urbanisation.
- After independence for exploitation of forest and mineral resources a number of industrial towns were established. They were also of heterogenetic origin and represented secondary urbanisation.
- The occupation of towns and city was based on non-agricultural occupation like service, business, trade, commerce, mining and industries.
- The population of towns and cities represented high density because a large number of people from villages have come to urban centres for work and livelihood.
- Urban centres have pluralities of culture, society, economy, religion and political organisations because people have brought cultures, religion and language with themselves.

- The environment of urban and industrial centres is not natural, rather is artificial.
- Caste association, linguistic associations, regional associations, religious associations and occupational associations exist in urban and industrial centres.
- In urban and industrial centres, people are free from caste system and caste occupations.
- Urban and industrial centres act as agent of social mobility.
- Social mobility in urban and industrial centres has led the establishment of class in place of caste in villages.
- Some castes such as washerman, leather worker, carpenters, potters, blacksmiths are found performing caste occupations, but on contract payment not on *Jajmani* relation.
- In urban and industrial centres formal social control is found through municipality, municipal corporation, administrators, *thana,* police and court.
- Urban and industrial society have formal interaction, impersonal relation and non-kinship relation.
- In urban and industrial society time is money and people spend money for holidays, entertainment in parks, markets, malls, restaurants, clubs etc.
- The civic amenities are provided to urban and industrial people.
- Villages and towns maintain continuous interaction.
- From the point of view of religion, many towns are centre of civilization. They have great traditions.
- The people of villages have little traditions but they have continuum with great traditional cities.
- The villages and towns show peasant urban continuum.
- A number of slums have emerged in towns, cities and metropolises.
- A number of social, cultural and economic problems are found in urban and industrial societies.
- For development of towns, cities and metropolises, town planning and programmes have been implemented.

6
Origin and Growth of City

From pre-historical researches, it has been established that man is a progressive animal. Man has made progress in different areas of life. On the basis of his experience, knowledge, technology and science he has been able to build his residence in villages, towns, cities, and metropolises. Now he is trying to settle in space. When man originated on this earth, he did not possess any kind of scientific knowledge. In those early times, he was bound to lead a life like wild animals. He was not a producer, he was consumer of things provided by nature particularly forest. He lived in caves or under or on big trees. He drank water from rivers or stream. He used to eat leaves, flowers, fruits and seeds available in jungle. He used to hunt animals and birds and do fishing. He used to wear leaves, barks and skin to cover body. Thus, his entire wants were fulfilled by nature. In this way, he spent his life as forest dweller, hunter and gatherer for several lakhs of years from lower Palaeolithic period to Mesolithic period. In Neolithic period, he gave rise to settled life and agricultural revolution. Now he became producer of fruits, grains and milk. He became village dweller by erecting houses. He began to domesticate animals and began to weave clothes. He discovered megalithic culture for burial purposes. He began to make pots. Thus, forest and band dwellers became village dwellers and cave dwellers became house dwellers.

After Neolithic period man entered in Chalcolithic Age and Bronze Age. In bronze age he gave birth to urban revolution. Around in 4000 B.C. in the river valley of Nile, Dajala, Farat and Indus, man became inhabitants of towns. He discovered town planning with specially designed buildings, roads and drainage system. He discovered numerals, accountancy and writing to keep records of trade and business. He discovered seals, established rules, and began to make payment to specialists like priest, carpenter, potter, coppersmith and bronzesmith and labourers involved in building towns and other works.

Causes of Origin of Towns

Production of copper and bronze, tools making from them and their use, discovery of plough, wheel, boat and bullock-kart were full of revolutionary possibilities. But without the reorganisation of society these discoveries were not so fruitful. Such evidences appeared from Cyria, Iran and Mediterranean and Baluchistan regions. Inhabitants of these regions were aware of all above inventions, but could not progress due to static social system. But in valleys of Nile, Dajala, Farat and Sindhu, situations were quite different. This great part of land was becoming more and more dry since early Holocene period. At that time mankind wanted to settle in such places where individual needs were fulfilled and which had sufficient water resources for irrigation and agriculture. Such environments were available in valleys of Nile, Dajala, Farat and Indus. Around 4000 B.C. suddenly population of mankind began to rise. With rise of population towns began to appear in those river valleys. These towns were too small in comparison to London, New York and Delhi, but they were too big in comparison to Chalcolithic villages. V. Gordon Childe has called this age as age of urban revolution.

Egypt is a small country surrounded by sea, mountain and desert. Its fertile land was created by flood soils of several thousand years. This land part has 30 feet thick layers of fertile soil. Its length is 750 miles and breath is 10 to 30 miles. In ancient period this part of land was so fertile that yields were taken thrice times in a year.

As Egypt is made up of flood soil brought by river Nyle, similarly Sumer is made up of flood soil brought by rivers Dajala and Farat. The land of Sumer was also known for its fertility in ancient times. The land was full of date plants and river. Tank and *jheel* were full of fishes. In this way, Egypt and Sumer both had attracted mankind to settle and build towns. In both those regions, rainfall was very low, but floods were very common. After flood, land became very hard. Hard labour was needed to develop them into a livable place. Without artificial means of irrigation, it was impossible to get success in agriculture. It was also necessary to control flood. It was also full of forest of reed. It was impossible for Chalcolithic small village to make a dam for controlling flood water, to make canal for irrigation and to clear the forest of reed. For these purposes, a big organisation of population was needed. Besides making dam and canal, it was also necessary to look after them regularly. That is why it had become essential for a big population to reside in organised way in Egypt and Sumer. The similar situation was also prevalent in Indus. Agriculturists of Egypt, Sumer and Indus had to produce more foodgrains, vegetables and milk to feed the larger population organisation in the form of cities. A number of specialists had emerged who were not involved in agriculture, but were dependent on agriculturists. They were priests, potters, carpenters, brass smith, bronze smith, mason, labourer, administrators, rulers and traders. There were trade relationship between Sumer, Egypt and Indus. Thus, these town-dwellers were interdependent on each other and agriculturists of their regions. This was very important for civil life.

In Sumer, foreign trade was in the hand of members of temple who were traders. Egypt also had traders as an independent class. Indus also possessed traders as an independent class. There were different trade centres where traders used to do export and import of required things. In order to provide protection to those traders, rulers of Egypt, Sumer and Indus had employed army. The king and rulers had established court to provide justice to traders, merchants, agriculturists and other classes and code of conduct was formulated. Temple priests and traders needed to keep records of trade and property. That is why, writing, accountancy, numerals, weight, measure and geometric laws were invented. The rise of towns gave rise to the development of script. With the development of script, it became possible to preserve knowledge of different kinds. In order to help agriculturists, solar calendar was discovered. Astrology and Astronomy were developed.

Seals were invented in order to provide symbols on things to be traded. Sealing and glazing technology was invented. When settling in towns, town-dwellers became attracted towards easy and luxurious life. They started erecting buildings in planned way with the help of unbaked bricks prepared in a frame and dried in sun. In the beginning of Chalcolithic age, man began to erect huts with the help of reed and soil. But in Indus Valley, town-dwellers had started erecting building with sun-baked bricks following road, street and drainage planning. The invention of bricks made possible to erect house and building of different designs. All such developments related to origin and growth of towns had taken place during Bronze Age. The urban revolution brought a change in the lifestyle of people. First of all towns originated in river valleys because at that time, the environments of river valleys were suitable for the origin and development of towns. The extension of these towns in both area and population was much more than the Chalcolithic villages. Mohenjodaro had an area of one square mile. The town of Sumer was spread over an area of 150 acres in which 24,000 people used to live. Lagas was a small town of Sumer, but had a population of 19,000 people. These towns had building of sun-baked bricks, fire-baked bricks and stone boulders. Towns of Indus had a well planned drainage, road and water supply. The sanitation and water arrangement of Indus was better than many middle age European towns. A number of Indian towns of today do not have such sanitation arrangement as that of Indus Valley towns. Agriculturists of these towns used such a plough and potters used such a wheel which were not replaced till the invention of industries. The economic base of these towns was foreign trade and business. Traders used to travel distant places with goods loaded on cattle, bullock-cart and boat. Traders of country and abroad were welcomed with all. They used to enhance the decoration of towns. Rulers of these towns felt pride in erecting palatial buildings, temples, canals, megaliths and extension of boundaries of the country. They used to engrave inscriptions on stone slabs, brass, bronze and copper plates.

In conclusion, we can say that in the early part of three millennium B.C., towns began to appear in River valley of Nyle, Dajala, Farat and Indus. Besides alphabets and iron tool inventions, all kinds of inventions related to urban life were invented in Bronze Age civilization.

Origin and Growth of Towns in Indian Context

As described earlier, in India towns were originated like Sumerian and Egyptian civilization in Indus Valley during Bronze Age.

Nearly 5,000 years before today, inhabitants of Indus Valley led the origin and foundation of urban civilization. These towns were Harappa, Mohenjodaro, Kalibangan, Chanhudaro, Lothal and Kot Diji. These Bronze Age towns were much bigger than Chalcolithic villages in area and population. Building multi-storey houses, labourers and other classes colonies, sanitation and drainage system, drinking water facility, great bath, fortified palace, and others threw sufficient light on the then Indian urban civilization. The economic life of Indus town inhabitants was based on specialization and localisation. Each trader used to do a particular type of business. The people of same occupation used to live in a separate colony together. This civilization was trade-based and it had trade relations with Egypt and Sumer.

Towns of Ancient India

In our sacred texts like Vedas, Puranas, *Mahabharata, Ramayana* and others, we find references about ancient Indian towns. In Buddhist and Jaina literatures, we also find references about ancient Indian towns. By 6th century B.C. we find references about 16 ancient states from Kashmir to Bengal. They were known as Mahajanpada. They were Kashi, Kaushal, Anga, Chedi, Magadha, Vijji, Malla, Vatsa, Kuru, Panchal, Matsya, Sursen, Ashmals, Avanti, Gandhar and Kamboj. A brief account of these ancient Indian states is being presented here.

Kashi

The Janapada of Kashi was located in south-eastern part of present day Uttar Pradesh state. Varanasi was its capital. This town occupied significant place in ancient towns of India. It was famous for its prosperity, trade-business and technology. It was also famous as a pilgrimage centre. In Vedas, the town is described as an abode of Lord Shiva and his consort Parvati. It is also known as town of Gods and Goddesses.

Kaushal

This Janapada was located in middle north part of present Uttar Pradesh state. In Epic age, its capital was Ayodhya, but in course of time, Shravasti had become its capital. From Buddhist literature, it appears that Shravasti was located on the bank of river Tapti and was very famous from the point of view of trade and commerce and prosperity. This town was located on ancient trade route.

Anga

The Janapada of Anga was located in the eastern part of Bihar state and included parts of Bengal, Jharkhand and Orissa. The town of Champanagar of present Bhagalpur was its capital. Champanagar was a famous centre of trade and business in those ancient times. It was a very rich town. It was also a centre of art, culture and civilization.

Chedi

This ancient Janapada was in southern part of India. Its capital was Shaktimati situated on the bank of river Cane. One finds reference about Shishupal as a great king of Chedi. Shishupal was killed by Lord Krishna of *Mahabharata*. A branch of this dynasty had entered in Orissa and established the state of Kalinga. Ashoka, the great, a Mauryan king had defeated the king of Kalinga.

Magadha

This was a very famous Janapada of ancient India. This ancient state was located around old Patna and Gaya districts of Bihar state. Its first capital was Rajgir, also known as Rajgriha and Girivajra Brihadaratha and Jarasandha were great king of this state. The Mauryan rulers had shifted its capital to Patliputra from Rajgir. During the rule of Bimbasara and Ajatshatru it had attained its maximum progress.

Vajji

In this Janapada eight small regions were included. Famous among them were Lichchavi, Videh and Gyatrik. The capital of Videha was Mithila, the capital of Lichchavi was Vaishali and the capital of Gyatrik was Kundalgram. Now, they are part of North Bihar.

Malla

It was a federal democratic state. In this state, there were two branches of Mallas—(i) Kushinagar branch, and (ii) Pawanagari branch. Probably Kasia near Gorakhpur was Kushinagar of ancient India and Padron, a place situated at a distance of 12 miles north was the Pawanagari. In Pawanagari Lord Buddha had shared his last food while in Kushinagar he had attained *moksha* (death).

Vatsa

This Janapada was located on the bank of river Yamuna in north-east direction from Chedi Janapada. Its capital was Koshambi situated at a distance of 80 miles from Allahabad. It was an important trade centre of ancient India.

Kuru

Under Kuru Janpada neighbouring regions of present Delhi and Meerut were included. Its capital was Indraprastha. It was probably Hastinapur of *Mahabharata.*

Panchal

This Janapada included some districts of modern Ruhelkhand. It was divided into two—(i) Northern Panchal, and (ii) Southern Panchal. The capital of northern Panchal was Ahichchatra and the capital of southern state was Kampilya. Draupadi of *Mahabharata* belonged to this state.

Matsya

This Janapada was located towards southern side of Kuru Janapda and western side of river Yamuna. Its capital was Viratnagar.

Sursen

This Janapada was located towards southern direction of Panchal Janapada. Its capital was Mathura.

Assak

This Janapada was located on the bank of river Godavari. Its capital was Potan or Potali. Later on, it was included in Avanti Janapada.

Avanti

The Malwa region of today was Avanti of ancient India. It had two parts—(i) Northern Avanti, and (ii) Southern Avanti. The capital of northern Avanti was Ujjaini and the capital of southern Avanti was Mahismati.

Gandhar

This Janapada was eastern part of present Afghanistan. Takshashila, Kashmir and west-northern states were included in it. Its capital was Takshashila. It had cultural and trade-related importance.

Kamboj

The name of Gandhar and Kamboj is taken together. It was a neighbouring Janapada of Gandhar Janapada. It was located towards north-western side of Gandhar. Its capital was Hatak or Rajpur.

Besides above mentioned ancient Indian towns, we find references of a number of towns in our sacred texts which were famous pilgrimage centres. They were Gaya, Prayagraj, Haridwar, Puri, Ayodhya, Kashi, Mathura, Somnath, Ujjain, Nasik, Auranga, Tirupati, Rameshwaram Badrinath, Kedarnath, Baijnathdham, Bhima Shankar, Vaishnav Devi, Ghrisneshwar, Traymbkeshwar, Nageshwar, Shaileshwar Vindhyachal and others.

Thus, in ancient India, the then rulers, kings, great kings had established towns as capitals, as trade centres throughout the length and breadth of ancient India.

Towns of Middle Age

During Middle Age, the Mughal rulers had established towns as capital, garden and tourist places. For example, Agra, Delhi, Jodhpur, Firozpur, Daulatabad, Fatehpur Sikri, Farrukhabad and others. They were administrative centres characterised by forts, temples, mosques, garden and palatial buildings.

Towns of British Period

When British Government was established in India, the British administrators established a number of towns as districts, commercial centres, seaport centres, industrial centres and army cantonment. Thus, from the point of view of industrialisation and administration towns were established in India during British period. The history of organised industrialisation in India is not very old. First of all, a cotton industry was established in

Bombay state in 1863. In 1921, Tata Steel Works was established. Before Independence capital towns, administrative towns, transport towns, seaport towns and army cantonment towns were established. Chitaranjan railway industry and Jamshedpur steel industry were established. Dehradun, Srinagar, Danapur, Ramgarh cantonment towns were established. Calcutta, Bombay and Madras were established as transport and seaport towns.

Towns of Independence Period

After Independence iron and steel, jute, sugar, cement, Dalda, cloth, paper, railway, fertilizers, glass industries were established in different states of our country. In the state of Jharkhand, Hatia, Bokaro, Jamshedpur towns came into existence due to steel industry. Dhanbad, Giridih, Muri, Ghatshila developed as mining towns. Rourkela in Orissa, Bhilai in Chhattisgarh, Durgapur in West Bengal, Salem of Tamil Nadu, Vijaynagar of Karnataka and Vishakhapatnam of Andhra Pradesh were developed due to establishment of steel industries. Calcutta was developed as Jute industry towns. Ahmedabad, Surat, Bombay and Indore developed as cloth industry. Sri Harikota developed as a science city and space technology city. Arms and ammunition industries have also been established. After Independence, there has been a considerable change in urban population in India. A decadal growth in urban population in India has been presented in the Table 6.1.

Table 6.1: Decadal growth of urban population in India (1901-2011)

Year	*Percentage of Urban Population*
1901	10.80
1911	10.30
1921	11.20
1931	12.00
1941	13.90
1951	17.30
1961	18.00
1971	19.90
1981	23.30
1991	25.70
2001	27.80
2011	31.15

Characteristics of Indian Urban Community

On the basis of 1971, 1981, 1991 and 2011 Census Survey, following characteristics of Indian urban communities have been determined:

- The urban community should possess essentially municipality, municipal corporation, cantonment board or notified town area committee.
- The urban community should have at least 5,000 population.
- 75 per cent male working population should have non-agricultural occupation.
- The density of population should have 400 per square kilometre.
- The urban community should have facility like housing colony and industrial area.
- The urban community should have school, hospital, road, water, electricity, transport and communication facility.

Table 6.2: Classification of Towns by Population Criteria

Class of Towns	*Population Criteria*
Metropolis	10,00,000 and above
Type I City	1,00,000 and above
Type II City	50,000–1,00,000
Type III Town	20,000–50,000
Type IV Town	10,000–20,000
Type V Town	5,000–10,000
Type VI Town	5000

Phase of Urban Development

The urban development has passed through following phases of development. They are as follows:

- 1st Phase
- 2nd Phase
- 3rd Phase (Metropolis)
- 4th Phase (Megalopolis)
- 5th Phase (Tyranopolis)
- 6th Phase (Nacropolis).

1st Phase

In the first phase of urban development, a village community is established. The development of agriculture and animal husbandry started along with establishment of village. Difference in occupational groups starts appearing such as agriculturists, labourer, carpenter, ironsmith, potters, barbers, priests and artisans. Primary groups start appearing and the village witnesses rise in population.

2nd Phase

In the second phase of urban development, general organisation of village takes place. Social organisation takes place on the basis of blood relation such as lineage, clan, caste, tribe and others. Through these organisations people feel secured. Each village has its own panchayat and own Gods and Goddesses. Agriculturists, artisans, priests and labourers interact with each other for different kinds of services and payment in kind or cash. Small industries of rice making, floor making, loaf sugar making, oil crushing, pottery making came into existence. Tradition, philosophy, education, art and music developed in the village. In this phase, a strong foundation for the development of town was provided by agriculture and allied work, small industries, trade, education, art, administration, road and transportation.

3rd Phase

In the third phase, places having more and more facilities of living and earning livelihood, attracted more and more population. This increased the density of population. The places having assumed means of irrigation, water resources and agricultural facility were turned into towns. A number of market centres were established to fulfil the needs of people. The villages came in contact with traders and traders came in contact with traders of other towns. This led to interdependence and interrelatedness. Traders and people began to interact with each other. This led to development of different types of inventions, education, and logical explanation. Logical explanation led to the development of science. People started thinking about things and re-evaluating them. This urban culture gave birth to a number of weaknesses and weakened the link of social relation. Conflict and competition arose. Social disorganisation and reorganisation took place

4th Phase

In this phase capitalist ideology took place and capitalist economy was established. Individuals became involved in earning more and more money. This led to industrial conflict and competition. Storage of money became the prime aim. Downfall of morality occurred. Capitalist became powerful. Exploitation and oppression came into existence. The importance of logic and science became important. Different types of culture appeared. People became materialist. Materialist thinking made them feelingless. They became selfish and social feelings were avoided. Social disorganisation and reorganisation took place. Capitalists and high class people sometimes started welfare work. The foundation of metropolis was laid in this phase.

5th Phase

In this phase, capitalist and class system attained its height. Conflict and competition became part of life. People became economically dependent on others. Corruption appeared and morality disappeared. Position and role of classes became clear. A gap was created in social, economic and political relation.

Unemployment and poverty increased. Unrest spread among people and crime increased. In order to press such behaviour dictatorship appeared.

6th Phase

In sixth phase, capitalist and individual became so down that they created pathological problems in towns. The entire society became meaningless. Social and economic organisation became valueless. Individual began to indulge himself or herself in different types of crime.

These six phases of urban development were explained by Mumford. But they were not applicable to all towns of all countries.

Causes of Urban Development

There is no doubt that density of population, fertile land of rivers and seas, army cantonment, industry and trade were nutritive factors for urban development. But a number of other factors had also contributed in the urban development time to time. For the purpose of study, we can divide urban development into two parts:

- Urban development in ancient period.
- Urban development in modern period.

Causes of Urban Development in Ancient Period

We can understand causes of urban development in ancient period in following ways:

Favourable Geographical Situation

A number of towns, cities and metropolises are seen on bank of rivers and seas. This throws light that towns and cities were developed on banks of rivers and seas. Geographical situations were favourable for the development of towns and cities during ancient period. The favourable geographical condition would have attracted people to come and settle on the banks of rivers or seas. Where after those were favourable conditions for agriculture, like fertile land, sufficient rainfall, cold and hot seasons, and means of irrigation people would have settled in small or big towns. Towns and cities were not developed on hills and in deserts during ancient period.

Agricultural Facility

During ancient period people established towns only in those areas which possessed favourable agricultural environment such as fertile land, means of irrigation and favourable seasons. That is why a good number of towns were established in plain areas during ancient time.

Means of Communication

There were no road and railway during ancient period for transportation of goods and for going and coming. They were bound to travel either on foot or through river ways. The people of ancient period did not select those places for establishment of towns which were not communicable easily through waterways. Rivers were only medium of transportation and communication. That is why people selected to establish town on the bank of rivers during ancient period.

Army Cantonment

In ancient period, India had hundreds of small states. Each state had its own army. They possessed big fort and army cantonment. In order to supply goods and services to kings, courtiers, army and others, people from different areas came and established towns by their respective residences. For example, Jhansi, Gwalior and Chittorgarh.

Capital

Capitals established by different ancient kings became towns in course of time. Being capital people were attracted to live there permanently because kings used to provide necessary facility to them. For example, Ayodhya, Mathura, Varanasi, Patliputra, Rajgir and others.

Places of Religious Importance

India had a number of religious towns since Vedic time. They were established as pilgrimage centres. People from different regions used to go there for pilgrimage and worship. These pilgrimage centres took the shape of town by a number of traders and businessmen settled there to provide facility to pilgrims, besides priests. For example Badrinath, Kedarnath, Puridham, Baijnathdham, Gaya, Prayag, Rishikesh, Haridwar, Tirupati, Ramesvaram, Nagarjun and others.

Educational Centres

In ancient times, a number of places were developed as educational centres. Those places as educational centres attracted students from India and abroad for education purpose. They were developed as towns in course of time. For example, Nalanda, Vikramshila and Takshashila.

Technological Centre

In ancient India, a number of places were famous as technological centres. They were developed into towns later on. For example, Kannauj, Moradabad, Firozabad and others.

Trade Centre

In ancient period, there were a number of trade centres in our country. They were situated on the banks of rivers and seas. They were developed as towns in due course. For example, Calcutta, Bombay, Madras, Puri.

Modern Causes of Urban Development

We can discuss modern causes of urban development under the following headings:

Industrial Revolution

Industrial revolution has played significant role in development of modern towns and cities. In towns and cities, a number of mills, factories and industries were established. For example. Iron industry, Steel industry, Jute industry, Paper industry, Cloth industry, Medicine industry, Chemical industry, Fertilizer industry, Leather industry, Sugar industry, Soap and Surf industry, Plastic industry, Furniture industry, Biscuits and Bread industry, Chocolate industry, Ice cream industry, Loaf sugar and sugar industry. In order to work in these industries, a good number of individuals came to perform work and duty at different levels and different time schedule. Residential colonies were made. Markets, schools, colleges, hospitals were established. In order to bring raw materials road and railway lines were made. Administration was established to look after the people and to provide facilities to them. In this way, industrial revolution was responsible for emergence of a number of towns and cities.

Development in Means of Communication

Means of communication connects one area with another area. Today we have roadways, railways, waterways, airways for carrying goods and passengers from one place to another. Developed means of communication save our time and money. The places having developed means of communication were developed as modern towns and cities.

Developed Means of Transmission

Developed means of transmission such as postal and telegraph, telephones, radio, newspapers, journals and others give us information about the places of trade, service and education. People from different parts of country go there for trade, work and employment. Thus, those places cause increase in population. Such places assume the shape of a town.

Increase in Population

Modern towns are created due to increase in population. Due to growth in population, a village turns in town, a town into city and a city into metropolis. Establishment of industries, office, market and enterprises, leads towards development of towns through rise in population.

Political Causes

Capitals of states and country have been created for political reasons to govern the people. Capitals attracted good number of people for work, employment, education and enterprises. In this way, modern towns like Delhi, Patna, Bubaneshwar, Bilaspur and other state capital towns emerged due to political reasons.

Urban Facilities

Urban facilities like road, drainage, street, electricity, education, sanitation, hospitals, employment and establishment of enterprises are urban facilities. They attract people of villages to come and settle in or nearby towns. In this way, modern towns develop.

Education Centre

Establishment of standard education institutions, colleges, university, technical and management institutes attract people to settle near those educational centres. Gradually residential colonies, business and market centres are established to supply goods to the people. In this way, educational centres assume the shape of a town.

Feeling of Safety

There is general feeling among the people that urban life is more secure than rural life. This feeling forces people to go and settle nearby towns to avail all modern facilities. Due to Naxalite movement and caste riots, people have come to settle in towns.

Agricultural Revolution

Now-a-days, agricultural revolution has been caused through machines like tractors and harvesters. HYV seeds, fertilizers, pesticides and chemical fertilisers have increased the yield.

In order to produce and supply those machines, HYV seeds, chemical fertilisers and to purchase agricultural produce, modern towns have come into existence.

Economic Attraction

The economic attraction of towns and cities invites people to come and settle in towns or cities from rural areas. Park, hotel, building, zoo, planetorium, cinema hall, glazing markets, fashionable dresses attract people of rural areas to come and settle in towns and cities.

Concept of Town

Town is such a community where one finds a mixed characteristics of urban and rural lifestyle. The town fulfils a number of needs of rural people. A town possesses the following features:

- Co-existence of rural and urban lifestyle.
- Intensity of industrialisation and marketisation.
- Market centre of neighbouring villages.
- Permanent residence of a big population.
- 5000 and above population.
- Establishment of Municipality.
- Notified area.
- Town area.
- Cantonment area.
- Road, electricity and water supply.

Concept of City

The life of city is crowded and full of activities. City has developed means of transportation, transmission and communication. It is a centre of business, trade and commerce. There are several means of entertainment. It also has a number of educational, religious and occupational institutions. A big population resides in city. City has municipal corporation to provide civil amenities to citizen. Individuals have formal relation. People do not know in detail about their neighbours. People maintain secondary relation.

It is very difficult to provide a definition of city community. Every people have a concept of city community as heterogeneity of ethnic groups, religious groups, occupational groups, market centres, educational centres and entertainment centres. It is also identified by plurality of cultures and lifestyle.

From the point of view of administration, a city is a place where a definite number of individuals reside in different colonies having a population more than 5000 to 1,00,000 governed by Municipality or Municipal Corporation.

From the point of view of ecology, a city is that place where people live in artificial environment. This environment is man-made not natural.

From historical point of view, a city is centre of civilization. From sociological point of view, city is a larger organisation of people having different ethnic, social, cultural, religious, political and lingual groups.

From anthropological point of view, a city is complex organisation of heterogeneous cultures followed by complex social, religious, political and lingual organisations.

Characteristics of City

Each city has its own identity and history of origin. Cities have different characteristics. But some common characteristics are found in all cities. They are as follows:

Non-agricultural Occupation

The occupation of city-dwellers is not based on agriculture and allied works. This is main point of difference between a village and a city. Here, main means of livelihood of an individual is service, labour, business, trade and entrepreneurship or enterprises.

Density of Population

The density of population of city is more than village. The residential colonies of cities are compact. Lakhs of people reside in one colony. That is why the density of population is very high in cities.

Extension of City

The population of a city go on increasing due to industrialisation and urbanisation. New trade and market centres come into existence. New residential areas are developed. Thus, extension of city takes place time to time.

Heterogeneous Population

A city is characterised by heterogeneous population having different castes, communities, classes and occupational groups.

Urban Form of Social Relation

The city has urban form of social relation. City-dwellers belong to different castes, religious groups, classes, occupational and linguistic groups. Thus, they show confluence of cultures. But people belonging to different cultural groups do not have sentimental feeling. The urban form of social relation has following characteristics:

Impersonal Relation

In cities individual-individual relation is not found. People live in neighbourhood, but do not know name, address and face of each other.

Formal Relation

In towns and cities people maintain formal relations. They live together but do not visit the house of each other without information. They do not have we-feeling. People visit in house of each other on birth, marriage and death ceremonies and festivals, but they maintain formal relation.

Individualistic Nature

In towns and cities, one finds the existence of individualistic nature. Every individual resides in the world of his/her own ego, desire and expectation. He/she makes attempts for his/her own pleasure, happiness, richness and wealthness. He/she does any kind of work to get his/her desire fulfilled. Here human value becomes secondary and individual value becomes primary.

Complex Social Relation

In town and city, individuals have to maintain complex social relationship. It is because here an individual is related not only to primary institutions, but a number of secondary institutions. In these secondary institutions his/her post and role are different. He/she may be head of family, chairperson of caste association, member of linguistic society, director of research institute, treasurer of teacher association, office bearer of political parties and others. Thus, he/she has to perform different kinds of role in different organisations and institutions. These show complex form of social relation.

Internal Organisation

Each town and city has its own internal organisations. These internal organisations show form of a town or city. They are as follows:

Place-related Internal Organisation

A town/city is organised internally in different small areas such as industrial area, market area, residential area, hospital area, administrative area, service area, transport area, railway area, tourism area, entertainment area, office area, tourist area, cantonment area, municipal area, sports area and parks area.

Internal Relations Related to Common Lifestyle

Town/city is a centre of heterogeneity. But town/city-dwellers have to follow some common lifestyle. For example, work hour, holiday, recess, opening and closing time of school, college, universities, markets, offices, courts, hotels, cinema halls, malls, bank, post-office, hospitals, hostels, lodges etc. Such functional unity is characteristic of urban lifestyle.

Residential and Structural Permanency

In town and city, colony, office, school, college, university, market centre, telephone exchange, radio station, television centre, hotel, hospitals, bus stand, railway station, airport, cinema hall, malls all have fixed place and permanent structure. They are not movable.

High Intensity of Mobility

Town and city have high intensity of mobility. Here an individual is free to move from one city to another related to service, business and trade. He/she is also free to leave one job or occupation and join another job and occupations.

Individual Life

In town and city people lead individual life. An individual does not meet and talk to his/her neighbours daily. On some specific formal occasions, he/she meets with neighbours.

Difference in Economic Structure

Town/city possesses difference in economic structure. Some people live in palatial buildings with all modern facility. On the other hand, some people live in slum and lead a life of starvation. They do not have any amenities.

Concept of Metropolis

From the point of view of population, a town/city having a population of ten lakh and above is known as metropolis or metropolitan town/city. The term metropolitan has its origin in Greek literature. In the beginning it was related to mother town *(Matrinagar)*. All ancient towns of Greek were based on this concept. These towns were organised on social, cultural, economic and political characters. In course of time, concept of high nationality was developed and those towns got extension. Present day Mahanagar has 10 lakh or more population, high nationality, multi-purpose work and international significance. Generally, metropolis gets its origin at those places which have scope of mega commercial centre. Metropolis is not combined within the boundary of a country. It is related to several countries. Metropolitan town has very high density of population and continuous extension. Metropolis has mega municipal corporation. This has very good and well road transport, rail transport, metro-rail and airways facilities. Communicational network is very good. Metropolitan cities have centres of national and international activities. According to 2011 census report, in our country there were 52 such towns which have population more than ten lakh. Calcutta is most populous cosmopolitan town. Other metropolitan cities are Delhi, Bombay, Madras, Bangalore, Hyderabad, Ahmedabad, Kanpur, Lucknow, Pune, Nagpur, Varanasi, Jaipur and others.

7
Concept of Urbanisation and Its Consequences

Concept of Urbanisation

Urbanisation is a process by which development of urban lifestyle takes place. This process was started in Bronze age and is still continuing. As a result of this process several small and big towns and cities have come into existence. Through this process, rural areas are transformed into urban areas. The process of urbanisation has given birth to urban community and urban culture. Although in process of urbanisation rural areas are transformed into urban areas, but urban areas have their distinct identity than rural area. They have urban style of life.

In order to understand the concept of urbanisation clearly, it is necessary to know the difference between town, urbanity and urbanism. It is because the process of urbanisation is closely related to the concept of town, urbanity and urbanism. A town/city is a community whose main means of livelihood is non-agricultural occupations. This community has all means of living a pleasurable and pleasantful life. The transport and communication system is very well developed. It has several institutions related to education, science, technology and medical science. Here, community members follow the rule related to working hours, rest and holidays. Modern and multi-storey structure are its speciality. People enjoy civil amenities.

Urbanity is a way of life. It is related to dress, ornaments, food behaviour, food habit, communication behaviour, relation behaviour, occupation behaviour and residential behaviour of people living in towns and cities.

Urbanism is an ideology on the basis of which attempt is made to know the origin and development of town/city and to support the development of towns for the development of people.

Urbanisation is process which is related to town, urbanity and urbanism.

Types of Urbanisation

American anthropologist Robert Redfield and Milton Singer, in their research papers (Cultural Role of City, 1954) have divided the process of urbanisation into two types:

They are as follows :

- Primary urbanisation
- Secondary urbanisation.

These two American anthropologists had attempted to know the development of urban culture and change in historical perspectives. According to them, towns have played significant role in development and change of urban culture which can be understood historically. They were of view that formation of a town was due to the process of acculturation adopted by folk and peasant society. Folk and peasant society as an ideal type represented a total of such social elements which are recognised as a homogeneous and non-literate community established in past. Such type of society is found in folk and peasant villages, not in towns. On the other hand, urban society as an ideal type represents such a community in which orthogenetic and heterogenetic transformation of folk and peasant society has occurred completely.

Orthogenetic transformation of folk and peasant society into an urban society has given birth to Great tradition and its special intellectual literary class. Due to this transformation, administrative official and laws came into existence. All these elements originated from material and religious life of local culture. Developed economic system also obeyed local cultural change. This in Redfieldian term is known as primary urbanisation.

Orthogenetic transformation of folk and peasant society made intellectual, aesthetic, economic and political life free from local moral values. This freedom led individuals attracted towards own desires and interests, on one hand. On the other hand, this freedom led the development of revolutionary native and humanistic approach. Reform, progress and designed change became possible due to this approach. This in Redfieldian term is known as secondary urbanisation.

Primary observation attains place as core culture which leads to development of a native urban civilization. Here, first of all acculturation of precivilized folk society takes place as a peasant society. The peasant society with its mixed culture gets attached to urban centre. In this process, first of all development of a religious culture takes place. This religious culture is termed as great tradition by urban literate class.

In secondary urbanisation, a precivilized folk and peasant society comes in contact with an urban society having different cultures. As a result, a new lifestyle is formed which is quite different from lifestyle of traditional or primary urban life. This urban lifestyle is opposite to traditional lifestyle.

No universal stage of primary and secondary urbanisation has been identified. But they have been formed by technical development and other cultural contact.

The result of primary urbanisation and secondary urbanisation has been important. The primary urbanisation has led to the development of great tradition. The expression of great tradition takes place in religious texts, architecture, images sculptured, temple erecting art, drawing art, building construction art and aesthetic values. Primary urbanisation becomes core of indigenous civilisation. Great tradition defines its moral, aesthetic, leagal and other cultural values through its own consciousness. Thus, great tradition becomes a source of religious, moral, aesthetic and cultural values. The rise of intellectual and literary class, here, has its own importance. The people of this class contribute significantly in the development of new ideas. New laws controlled by local cultures come in existence. The distribution of resources in economic areas occur as per traditional status and moral laws. This is true for production and distribution both. Thus, in primary urbanisation coordination of political, economic, intellectual and aesthetic activities takes place through great tradition.

In secondary urbanisation such a mentality is created which

does not coincide with local culture. Such situations may be as follows:

- A proper adjustment through favourable technological system.
- Development of common feeling towards groups.
- Origin of different groups having different backgrounds.
- Development of a relative importance approach in place of pre-effective approach.

Thus, in secondary urbanisation, different aspects of system develops independently, not as per great tradition. But in primary urbanisation different aspects of system develop as per great tradition and maintain their existence.

Examples of Primary and Secondary Urbanisation in India

In the history of mankind, urban civilization has its own importance which started in Bronze age and has been continuing even today. On the land of the then India urban centres like Mohenjodaro, Harappa, Chanhudaro, Kalibangan and Lothal appeared in Bronze age. Thereafter, a number of towns appeared in Vedic age. They were Gaya, Ayodhya, Mathura, Dwarka, Kashi, Allahabad, Puri, Rameshwaram, Tirupati, Somnath, Haridwar and others. These towns were originated as either religious centre or as religio-administrative centre. These towns were developed as per values of great tradition. The great tradition of these towns got expressions in scared texts, art, architect, drawing and aesthetic value. Moral, religious intellectual, aesthetic, legal and cultural values were developed according to the value of great tradition. Thus, these towns were orthogenetic in origin and were good examples of primary urbanisation. Due to primary urbanisation, such towns were developed whose entire system was based on great tradition. These primary urban centres played significant role in bending the people of a region and sometimes whole country through its great traditional behaviour. They were also responsible for development of nationalism in ancient Indian people.

Town formation is a continuous process. In Middle Age, Mughal rulers developed a number of towns such as Delhi, Agra,

Daultabad, Firozpur, Farrukhabad, Fatehpur Sikri, Aurangabad, Sasaram etc. These towns were not of religious origin. They did not have any great traditions. These towns were developed as symbols of capital, memory, garden, palace and art and architecture.

When British came to India with developed science and technology, they led the formation of a number of towns as capital, districts, army cantonment, transport, trade and commerce centres. The most significant contribution of British period was establishment of machines and industries. Thus, a number of towns came into existence due to establishment of industries.

After Independence, our Government followed the policy of establishing different kinds of industry such as Sugar, Cement, Paper, Surf, Soap, Dalda, Chemical fertilizer, Aluminium, Copper, Brass, Cloth, Jute, Leather, Arms and Ammunition, Railway, Iron, Steel, Medicine, Food items and others. As a result, towns, cities and metropolises have come into existence. Nearly 30 per cent people of our country have become urban-dwellers. Towns and cities developed due to mining, industrial, administrative, trade, business and commercial causes were heterogenetic in origin. They were not orthogenetic in origin. They are termed as example of secondary urbanisation in Redfieldian terminology. Here system is not developed according to moral and religious value of a great tradition. Rather system is developed on the basis of secular approach. These towns were developed free from values of great tradition. Due to freedom from great tradition revolution, progress and development took place in town emerging due to secondary urbanisation. People were attracted towards individual needs and development of indigenous and humanistic approach was followed.

Difference between Primary and Secondary Urbanisation

Primary Urbanisation	*Secondary Urbanisation*
1. In primary urbanisation process, urban society has emerged due to orthogenetic transformation of folk and peasant society.	1. In secondary urbanisation process urban society has emerged due to heterogenetic transformation of folk and peasant society.
2. Primary urbanisation is concerned with traditional towns.	2. Secondary urbanisation is concerned with modern town.
3. Primary urbanisation develops great traditional towns.	3. Secondary urbanisation develops complex modern lifestyle towns.

(*Contd.*)

Primary Urbanisation	*Secondary Urbanisation*
4. In primary urbanisation, the expression of great tradition occurs through sacred texts, art, architecture, drawing, aesthetic scenes, priests, mythology and legend.	4. In secondary urbanisation, the expression of modern complex lifestyle occurs through individualism, independent view, work and holiday culture, formal relation, selfishness and time is money culture.
5. The primary urbanisation has given birth to sacred culture.	5. The secondary urbanisation has given birth to secular culture.
6. In primary urbanisation process, entire social, economic, political, religious and cultural systems are governed by values of great tradition.	6. In secondary urbanisation, entire social, cultural, economic political and religious system is governed by secular approach.
7. Morality occupies prime place in primary urbanisation.	7. Morality does not occupy prime place in secondary urbanisation.
8. Primary urbanisation brings folk and peasant society in interaction with great tradition.	8. The secondary urbanisation forces folk and peasant society to go and migrate for various purposes.
9. Primary urbanisation establishes interaction between little tradition and great tradition.	9. Secondary urbanisation establishes occupational and marketing relation between folk and peasant society and urban society.
10. Primary urbanisation has developed regional and national culture.	10. Secondary urbanisation has developed unionism and political participation.
11. Primary urbanisation develops traditional urban style of life.	11. Secondary urbanisation develops modern urban style of life.
12. Primary urbanisation develops philosophical approach.	12. Secondary urbanisation develops humanistic approach.
13. Primary urbanisation has developed the concept of pilgrimage centre.	13. Secondary urbanisation has developed educational, knowledge and science centres.
14. It is related to indigenous culture and civilization.	14. It is related to external culture and civilization.
15. In primary urbanisation economic division takes place through status and moral value.	15. In secondary urbanisation, economic division takes place on the basis of expertise, ability and qualification.

Impact of Urbanisation

We can discuss the impact of urbanisation under following headings:

- Social Impact of Urbanisation
- Economic Impact of Urbanisation
- Religious Impact of Urbanisation

- Political Impact of Urbanisation.

Social Impact of Urbanisation

The social impact of urbanisation can be discussed under following sub-headings :

Disorganisation of Joint Family

The urbanisation has influenced the structure system of family system. Rural society is characterised by joint family system. But those members who have come in urban centres for work and employment, have established nuclear family in towns. They visit their villages on some occasions of festivals and ceremonies. They make frequent visit in early days of settlement in town. But work load and education of children compel them to remain in towns. This tendency gradually leads to disorganisation of joint family system.

Existence of Plural Society

In towns, an individual has to live in plural society having different castes and religious groups. He/she and his/her family members have to make adaptation according to plural societies.

Cultural Exchange

The urbanisation has forced people to make cultural give and take. A town/city has complex network of culture of different ethnic, religious and lingual groups. People make exchange of cultural traits. Here people adopts dress, food, language, and ways of life of other people. Urban centres present a situation of cultural pluralism. In Delhi people adopt Punjabi and Haryanavi culture. In Mumbai Marathi culture, in Ahmedabad Gujarati culture, in Bhubaneswar Oriya culture, in Calcutta Bengali culture, in Banaras, Banarasi culture, in Lucknow Lakhnavi culture, in Patna Bihari culture. Thus, in towns and cities cultural exchange takes place among people.

Change in Social Values

In urban centres change in social values has taken place. Towns have become symbols of progressive culture. Here, people are influenced greatly by education, science and technology.

A number of traditional beliefs and blind faiths are being not accepted on the basis of science, education and technology. In place of social values emphasis is being placed on individual values. Here individuals do every thing for him/her benefit, but not for the benefit of society.

Decrease in Orthodox Religion

In urban society traditional values are getting broken. People are gradually leaving belief in *Puja-Path* or adopting them in simple way. Performance of lengthy rituals are decreasing. Here people of different religions work together, live together, eat together and talk together. As a result religious fanaticism is decreasing. Here people do not want to get attached with old tradition and accept traditions of blind faith.

Decrease in Family Control

The control of family on family members is decreasing. Here a family member works freely.

Change in Social Relation

In towns and cities, social relation is formal. Here, people fulfil formality in maintaining social relation with neighbour, friend, kin, and occupational groups. People visit in the house of each other after getting invitation and that too for some time and return home after few hours. They make exchange of gifts and visits to fulfil formality. Here, formality in social relation is more and ownness is less.

Change in Status of Woman

Due to urbanisation, a change in status of women has taken place. They are free from maintaining *Parda Pratha*. They have emerged as leaders and entrepreneurs. This has brought a positive impact on status of women in towns and cities.

Tolerance

Urbanisation has developed tolerance in people. Here each individual and family is alone in a big crowd of urban population. He/she has to face all problems alone. He/she has to face joy and sorrow, poverty and richness, praise and defame alone. As a result, individual develops tolerance in his/her behaviour.

Commercialisation of Entertainment

In towns and cities sale and purchase of entertainment takes place. In towns and cities hostels, clubs, restaurants, theatre, cinema hall, parks, planetorium and others are means of entertainment. People have to pay for entertainment at these places. The rich people enjoy entertainment by paying more and more money. People do not gather for *Bharat Natyam* and *Kathak* dances, but for modern dances they make more payment and gather in a crowd. They pay more for naked dances. Youth are more attracted towards nakedness and commercialisation of entertainment.

Economic Impact of Urbanisation

Modern towns and cities are based on economic resources. Economic development and progress has influenced the entire life of individuals in towns and cities. Urbanisation has made individuals progressive, individualistic, competitive, opportunists and goal achievers. The economic impact of urbanisation can be discussed under following sub-headings:

Increase in Trade and Commerce

The emergence of towns and cities have opened a number of opportunities for market, trade, commerce and business. It is because a town or city is a centre of trade and industries. Here, an individual finds a number of alternatives for jobs and business. An individual is free to select job or opt business. Job is based on educational qualification and ability. Therefore, every individual cannot get job. But choice of business is left for both educated and uneducated. Keeping consumers in mind people opt business. In towns, majority of people are engaged in business and own enterprises.

Money is Life

A town or city revolves on an axis of money and individuals rotate around money. From morning to evening people want to earn money more and more. Here, money is everything. Money determines relation and status. Money becomes a cause for breaking a relationship. It also becomes a cause for establishing relationship. Here, there is no value of an individual. Here everybody values money. They worship money not mother and father.

Here, a characterful individual is avoided and neglected. But characterless individuals, black marketeers, corruption doers, and white collar criminals are welcomed, valued and respected. Due to rise and fall in market, business doers want to earn more and more in very short time. This has increased corrupt practices in towns and cities.

Production of Adulterated Goods and Extended Market

In towns and cities, business doers attempt to become rich by producing adulterated goods which are termed as two number not one number goods. The main purpose behind adulteration is to earn more and more. For this purpose, they have extension of market. They want to sell their adulterated goods more and more in extended market.

Inequality in Economic Area

Towns and cities have been a centre of economic inequality. On one hand people live in palatial buildings, multi-storey buildings, 5 star hotels and air conditioned rooms, but on the other hand people live in slums where there are no civic amenities. One finds crowds of beggars, unemployeds, hungers, poors and prostitutes, who are bound to face exploitation, oppression and deprivation.

Impact on Political Life

Urbanisation has influenced the political life of people. Towns and cities have become arena of different political parties, unions, associations, activists and civil society. The impact of urbanisation on political life of people can be discussed under the following sub-headings:

Political Awareness

In towns and cities people are aware of their rights and duties. They participate in political activities. They struggle for their rights. They are so conscious that they organise bund, go on strike, lead protests and set on fast unto death or hunger strike. Here people organise easily against unjustice. In order to get justice, they visit court for justice.

Political Activism

Urbanisation has led to activism among people. Urban people are more active in nation building. They opine freely on national and international issues. Here, men and women both are active in different fields. Women are chairperson of municipal corporation and political parties.

Impact on Caste System

Urbanisation has influenced the functioning of caste system. The impact of urbanisation on caste system can be discussed under following sub-headings:

Decrease in Feeling of Untouchability

The urbanisation has played significant role in removing the practice of untouchability. Today Brahmin and *Dalit* work together in office, live together in colony, eat together in hostels and restaurants, travel together in bus, train and aeroplane, and participate in joys and sorrows in towns and cities. Such practices have reduced the feeling of untouchability.

Change in Traditional Work

Urbanisation has played significant role in changing the caste-based traditional occupation. Here an individual belonging to any caste is free to select jobs or business of any type. A *Dalit* is free to educate himself or herself and select job on the basis of qualification. He/she is also free to select a business such as hotel, shops, cloth store, grain store and others. Here, a washerman is not supposed to washing of cloths, a shoe maker is not supposed to do shoemaking. He/she may establish laundry or a shoe store or may select other types of business. Thus, urbanisation has made transformation in caste-based traditional occupations.

Decrease in Caste, Religion and Culture

Urbanisation has played significant role in decreasing caste-based religion and culture. Here an individual becomes above caste. He/she is not bound to perform all rituals related to a particular caste. He/she may change his religion. He/she can perform worship or not.

Inter-Caste Marriage

Urbanisation has increased the incidence of inter-caste marriages. The urbanisation has provided boys and girls of different castes and religion to study together and to work together and to do same status jobs. Such types of conduct in educated and employed boys and girls is leading towards inter-caste marriages. Such marriages are getting acceptance of the urban society.

From above account, it is quite clear that urbanisation has brought a number of positive impact on life and culture of people living as an urban community. But it has also brought a number of negative impacts on life of people. It has given birth to a number of social pathological problems like poverty, unemployment, prostitution, beggars, corruption, adulteration, admixture, white collar crimes, immorality, drinking habit, juvenile delinquency and slums. These problems are leading towards personality and social degradation.

8
Concept of Industrialisation and Its Consequences

Industrialisation is a process by which industrial urban life style is created. But industrialisation has been taken as a model of development by all countries of the world. It has reduced the pressure on agricultural land and provided opportunities to the people for jobs and, business and market. Thus, it has been used as a means to reduce poverty. Because without proper and full use of resources, development and prosperity cannot be thought and hoped. This model of development was not only introduced by British government, but also by our Prime Minister, Pt. Jawaharlal Nehru after Independence. He had laid the foundation of a number of mega industrial complexes in our country for the purpose of development. That is why the industrialisation after Independence is also known as Nehruisation in our country.

Industrialisation is that way by which any country of the world can do maximum use of its economic, natural and technological resources for its development. On one hand, the standard of life can be raised by it, on the other hand, a number of demerits of economy can be removed. It makes economy strong. That is why all countries of the world have accepted the process of industrialisation. It not only makes a change in economy of the country, but it is also responsible for social, cultural and religious changes.

Today, it is being propagated that the world has entered in the stage of post-industrialisation through science, knowledge and technology. The process of globalisation has replaced the process of industrialisation and mechanisation. After 1990, the world has achieved post-industrial stage through knowledge revolution. Where industrialisation was concerned with British imperialism and mechanisation, the globalisation is concerned with multinationalism through knowledge and information technology. Now, attempts are being made to produce knowledge and information related apparatus in place of production of goods of different kinds. Where industrialisation provided jobs to thousands of people, but globalisation utilities services of only knowledge workers, who do the work of several people through a single computer. Where industrialisation had not made individuals saleable, the globalisation has made individual salelable.

Industrial Revolution

During 16th century, Europe witnessed scientific revolution. Scientific revolution gave rise to mechanisation and industrialisation. As a result, Europe witnessed industrial revolution in 18th century. Industrial revolution is basically gift of England. This revolution gave rise to internal inventions. It provided efficiency to produce more in less time. A machine began to perform work of several individuals. First of all Kartrite had made a machine which worked through water. With the help of this machine, a 15 years old boy could perform the work equivalent to 15 persons. In 1750, coal stone was discovered. This increased the efficiency of machine more. In 1765, James Watt invented steam engine. This provided energy and intensity to industrial revolution. Now, a number of mechanical inventions were made one after the other. The new mechanical inventions gave rise to such a new age in the history of mankind which is known as industrial age.

In India industrial revolution took place in British rule. This revolution got momentum during Prime Ministership of Pt. Jawaharlal Nehru. During Muslim rule industries of paper, colour, explosive materials, matchbox, bangles etc. were established. But they were not organised industries. The organised industry in India in the form of Jute Mill came into existence in 1853 in Bombay province. Till First World War, only industries of Jute, Cotton and Coal were established in India. Tata Steel Works industry was established in Jamshedpur in 1921. The reason behind this slow industrial progress in India was politics of that time in our country. The main aim of East India Company was to propagate its own trade in India, not in establishing more and more industries in India. Following this policy raw materials were brought in England from India and goods produced in England were brought to India for selling among people.

From Bangbhang movement of 1905 and Swadeshi move Indian industries had got some encouragement. Swadeshi goods were preferred by the people and their demands were on increasing. In 1916, Industry Commission was formed. Through commission, only those industries were encouraged which could produce iron, steel and chemicals to be used in war. In the period between First and Second World War, the situation of industrial development remained neglected. The country had to face great loss. After end of World War, the legacy of country was very troublesome. Prices of goods were increased. Troubles were faced in getting machines and their parts. Labourers were scrutinised at great level. Political and communal revolutions were increased. Turmoil prevailed in entire country. The industrial development witnessed a jolt. A number of other troubles also arose.

After Independence, our Government through five year plan brought small and medium scale revolution. Previously machines and parts were brought from foreign countries. But now-a-days we have been able to produce machines and their parts in our own country. Today, we are also exporting own produced machines and their parts to other countries.

Definition of Industrialisation

The term industrialisation can be defined in narrow sense and broad sense both. In narrow sense, the meaning of industrialisation is to establish more and more manufacturing industries for production of more and more goods to be sold in market so that the standard of life of people could be raised.

In broad sense, industrialisation means industrial organisation based on latest scientific knowledge and technology so that large scale capital could be invested for production, distribution, exchange, trade and market.

From above both definitions, we can say that industrialisation is such a process by which industries are established on the basis of latest modern scientific knowledge and technology for the purpose of production of goods to improve economic resources and raise the standard of living of people.

Modern Tendency of Industrialisation

The modern tendencies of industrialisation are as follows:

Technical Progress

The industrial revolution has been brought in the world by technical change. All countries of the world want to gain latest technical knowledge so that more and more qualitative goods could be produced in less and less investment.

Planned Industrialisation

Previously industries were established in unplanned way. But now-a-days, industries are established in planned way.

Productivity Movement

The process of industrialisation has been enhanced through productivity movement. Every country wants to produce more on less investment.

Government Cooperation

The government has also played significant role in growth of industries. Our government has encouraged both public sector industries and private sector industries.

End of Monopoly

Today, there is no monopoly of any one country in establishment of industries. Rather all countries of the world have adopted the policy of industrialisation. In this way, monopoly has come to an end.

Impact of Industrialisation

The impact of industrialisation can be discussed under the following headings:

- Impact on Family Life
- Impact on Social Life
- Impact on Economic Life.

Impact of Industrialisation on Family Life

Industrialisation has influenced the family life. We can discuss the impact of industrialisation on family life under following sub-headings:

Birth of Nuclear Family

Process of industrialisation has given birth to nuclear family. It is because industrialisation is not suitable for joint family system. People from villages come to work in industries. They also bring their family. They began to live in separate quarters meant for them. Gradually, the division of joint family took place. The people of villages spread in different industrial towns for work. Thus, joint family system of villages got disintegrated and nuclear family came into existence.

Distance between Office and House

In villages people work in houses or in their fields. They had their own house and field. The workplace was same village. But workers of a factory live in quarters built away from factory site. They have to go to factory to perform work there which is popularly termed as duty. Duty hours remain of eight hours. They have to travel miles and miles to visit factory site and perform duty. They use bicycle, scooter, motorcycle, auto-rickshaw, bus to visit the factory. In Mumbai and Calcutta people have to cover a distance of 70-80 km per day to attend duty and return home. They visit factory by train or buses. This influences the family life of workers.

Decrease in Family Control

Industrialisation has made both husband and wife as workers. They have to leave home at a fixed time and come back home on a fixed time. Children of such parents feel neglected. The structure of family is nuclear. There are no old persons in the house to look after children. Husband, wife and children live without any control of guardianship. In this way, industrialisation has decreased the control in family of industrial society.

Individualistic Philosophy

The industrialisation has caused the development of individualistic philosophy. Individualistic philosophy has caused hurt to the feelings of joint family and made it disintegrated. The individual has made him/her master of house. He/she lives in house erected by himself/herself. He/she does not care for neighbour and society. He/she has himself/herself approach of life, family neighbour and society.

Impact on Daily Routine

The industrialisation has brought impact on daily routine of family of workers. All members of a family follow the time table of factory. They leave bed, have breakfast, go to factory, perform duty, come back home and go to bed as per the routine set by the factory. Family members meet each other together on holidays and go out for entertainment.

No Division of Labour in Family

Due to industrialisation, division of labour according to age and sex has disappeared. Here, husband and wife both are employed. Therefore, they cook together, they finish the work of kitchen and room cleaning together and take care of children together. Domestic work is not female specific or male specific. There is full cooperation of husband and wife in performance of household work. Now, they do the work of room cleaning through vacuum cleaner and clothes with washing machines. They cooperate with each other.

Change in Work Area of Woman

Industrialisation has made a change in the work areas of women. Now, their work area is not confined to house. They have put their feet outside house for work. They are engaged in service, business and enterprises. They have to go office for performing jobs and business. For this purpose, they have to travel miles and miles. They travel by train, bus, car, taxi, auto-rickshaw and own scooter. They are discharging their duties successfully with full responsibility, whether the post is small or big.

Change in Status of Woman

Industrialisation has brought changes in the status of women. Now, women are not only house-wife. They are studying and gaining knowledge of different kind. They are serving big or small posts, sharing the burden of family business, starting own business and entrepreneurship. They are contributing significantly in family income. They are now not liability, but asset for the family. Now, they are enjoying high status in the society. They are welcomed in family. Their names are taken with respect in family and society. Now they are not treated as machine for producing children and performing works in family from dawn to dusk. On the basis of education, knowledge and hard labour, they have raised their status high in the society.

Love Marriage and Inter-caste Marriage

The industrialisation has caused the formation of family based on love marriage and inter-caste marriage. Industries and factories attract boys and girls for employment and work. Young boys and girls work together in industries. They live together in colony. They develop love relation which gradually takes the form of love marriage and inter-caste marriage. The love marriage has caused inter-caste and inter-religious marriage.

Change in Marriage Age

Industrialisation has made a change in marriage age of boys and girls. The industrialisation had made boys and girls career-oriented. After getting higher education they want to arrange marriage. Job has become the first choice. In study and getting jobs, they attain age of 25 to 30 years or even more.

Occurrence of Divorce

Industrialisation is causing divorce in family. Husbands and wives both are in jobs. Both are economically interdependent. They are tied as couple through love. There is no one in family to exercise control over couple. After marriage, real truth of family life appears. They do not make compromise. They do not adapt with each other as couple. As a result, they decide to seek divorce. Thus, in industrial towns, one finds a number of single parent family.

Decrease in Religious Value

The industrialisation has caused decrease of religious value in family day by day. A family is centre of religious activities. In family religious values are taught in the form of sin, charity, good work, bad work, heaven and hell. But the working couple treat earning money as their religion. They do not believe in *Pap*, *Punya*, good work, bad work, heaven, hell, *Dharma* and *Adharma*. On the basis of science and logic they discard religious values—worship of Gods, ancestral Gods and Goddesses are part and parcel of family life. But families of industrial society are not practicing religious values.

Decrease in Sex Morality

Industrialisation has decreased sex morality in industrial society. Due to service and occupation husband and wife live separately at two different places and perform different jobs. They have to live in physical separation. They do not find sufficient time to meet with each other. As a result, they start taking alcohol and some of them develop extramarital relation. As husband and wife live separately, they do not exercise control over children. They become victim of juvenile delinquency. Unemployment in second generation of workers has also caused decrease in sex morality.

Impact of Industrialisation on Social Life

The industrialisation has influenced the social life of workers. The impact of industrialisation on social life of workers can be discussed under the following sub-headings:

Distance from Nature

The process of urbanisation has caused the development of industrial towns. In industrial towns, the social life of workers have become far away from nature. Here, nature has confined itself to factories, smokes, buildings, colonies, school, hospital, market and multi-storey buildings. Here people and family members do not get time and chance to sit under a tree on green grass and breath fresh air. They are bound to breath polluted air and live in artificial environment. They have to face the problem of not only air pollution, but also of water pollution and sound pollution. People live in air conditioned rooms with well-decorated curtains, sleep in late night and get up quite late after sunrise. The life of workers remain away from nature. This has influenced the social life of people.

Artificial Behaviour

Industrialisation has created artificial behaviour in family and society of workers and other people living in industrial towns. Here, individuals do not behave in natural manner. They behave in artificial manner. The artificial behaviour is also known as formal behaviour. Here individual visit in the house of others to meet on phone appointment, have smiling face at the time of meeting, say sir/madam, or hello-hi, shake hands, occupy seat as per instruction, ask the cause of meeting, share tea and then return. They say good bye at the time of returning. These are not our natural behaviour. These are our artificial or formal behaviour. Here, people become accustomed of artificial behaviour.

Individualistic Approach

Industrialisation has developed individualistic approach in industrial urban society. Here, individuals are moving far away from spiritual thinking. The tendency of satisfaction in little has vanished. Individuals are attracted towards wealth and property, not towards society. The wealth and property has become primary thing and society has become secondary thing. The role of wealth and property has increased and social and religious values have decreased. Post and position are determined by wealth not by spirituality. People have been attracted towards lust and passion not in social service.

Appearance of Slums

Industrialisation has caused emergence of slums. Industrialisation has attracted a good number of labourers from rural area to do work and earn wages in cash. Their number is increasing day by day. They do not get house to live. They erect huts or tents nearby factory area, bus-stand, railway station, port, by the side of roads and other fields. In this way slums appear in industrial areas. In a small hut, or room, a number of individuals accommodate. A bed sheet and net become the bed for a couple. Here, individuals do not avail civic amenities. They start sharing alcohol, playing gambling and other immoral acts related to sex. Such pathological problems affect the social life of industrial urban society.

Birth of New Diseases

Industrialisation has given birth to a number of diseases in industrial urban society. Industrialisation has caused air pollution, water pollution, soil pollution and sound pollution. Pollution caused by industrialisation is responsible for sugar, B.P., gastritis, heart, lungs, eye, ear and other kinds of diseases. Uncontrolled sex relations are giving birth to a number of sex related diseases.

Sale and Purchase of Entertainment

Industrialisation has caused sale and purchase of entertainment. People want to enjoy Sunday and other state and national holidays. They visit park, cinema, mall, restaurant, planetorium, museum and zoo. They pay money and buy ticket. The tickets are sold at different rates. People purchase ticket according to money in their pockets. People visit dance club, beauty parlour and other places where entertainment are sold and purchased.

Gambling, Wine and Sex Immorality

The industrialisation has enhanced the play of gambling, taking of wine and having pre-marital and extra-marital relation. When workers come to perform work in industries do not bring family with themselves. They come first alone. All workers do not get quarters. They have to share quarter or hire on rent. In absence of family, they become indulged in gambling, drinking wine and sex immorality. Some have to face the problem of personality disorganisation and social disorganisation.

Population Explosion

Industrialisation has caused population explosion in industrial urban area. The rise in population has created a number of problems such as unemployment, theft, snatching, dacoity, murder, beggary and sexual immorality.

Male-Female Ratio in Population

Industrialisation affects the sex ratio of industrial urban population. From villages people come without family and children. Low salary, not certainty of work regularly and temporary jobs do not allow them to bring family. Thus, they live alone. This practice influences the sex ratio of industrial urban centres. Imbalance in sex gives rise to a number of pathological problems.

Downfall of Community Life

Due to industrialisation downfall of community life has occurred. There is no we-feeling among members of community. People do not participate in community programme wholeheartedly. They give contribution and become free. The urban life has kept the people limited to a cup of tea. People share tea, breakfast, food, perform worship and visit different places individually. They do not do anything collectively. It is because they have 'I-feeling' in place of 'we-feeling'.

Conflict and Competition

Industrialisation has made people individualistic and competitive. They want to progress even at the cost of others. This tendency creates conflict. Not only workers, but industrialists and traders are also competitive. Because on the basis of competition one industrialist moves ahead of other industrialists. In competition, some becomes rivals. Conflict arises between them which ends in murder and other types of crime. For success, they forget due-undue and moral-immoral.

Crime and Juvenile Delinquency

Industrialisation has given birth to a number of crimes and juvenile delinquency. A number of organisations and institutions of towns have given birth to crime. For example, quarrel in life, struggle, competition, unemployment and slums.

Educational Progress

Industrialisation has caused progress in education. Industrial towns have a number of institutions of higher education, engineering, medical, management, commercial education and technical education. Such education has created more and more intelligentsia.

Birth of New Value

Industrialisation has created a number of new values. Values have been added according to salary and posts. If a low caste person achieves a high post, he/she enjoys high value in society. He/she is not treated as untouchables. Rather he/she is addressed as sir and madam. People accept food and water gladly without any hesitation. He/she is respected everywhere. Today seeing T.V. serials with aged and parents are not taken as bad. Dancing with other women in club is not taken bad. Having female friends and male friends are not taken bad. Seeing modern dances with family in dance centre is not taken bad. In fashion, semi-nakedness is also accepted. Taking wine with wife is also not taken as bad. Thus, industrialisation has added a number of new values in industrial society.

Impact of Industrialisation on Economic Life

The industrialisation process has influenced economic life of industrial urban society to a great extent. Impact of industrialisation on economic life can be discussed under following sub-headings:

Importance of Capitalism

Industrialisation has added value to capitalisation. In industrial society, money and wealth is regarded as blessing of Gods and Goddesses. They are worshipped like deities. People enchant mantra, and offer flowers and *Agarbatti* to the place where money is kept in house. God and Goddess of wealth Lakshmi and Ganesh are worshipped daily and on the occasion of Deepawali with great devotion and preparation. Along with Goddess Lakhsmi, Goddess Saraswati and Goddess Durga are also worshipped. Goddess Saraswati is worshipped for good education and good employment. Goddess Durga is worshipped for good flow of energy in body so that he/she could enjoy the prosperous life. God Vishvakarma is worshipped for technological advancement and qualitative production in industries. Thus, industrial society value too much on money. Here, money measures human relation. An individual attains respect by weighing in balance of money too much propertied and wealthy attain too much respect.

Rise of Classes

The industrialisation has created two important classes: (i) Capitalist, and (ii) Labourer. Besides these two industrial classes, traders, businessman and intelligentsia also reside in industrial urban town. On the basis of income town dwellers are divided into three classes—(i) Lower income group, (ii) Middle income group, and (iii) High income group.

Specialisation of Work

In units an individual cannot perform all types of work by himself. Here each type of work is performed by a separate machine run by an expert individual. Different types of machines have created different types of employment. Here there are diversities of machines, works and experts. Thus, industrialisation has created specialisation of work.

Unemployment

Industrialisation has also caused the problem of unemployment. All industries do not run round the year. They work only for few months in a year. Some industries become ill and do not restart. Thus, industrialisation creates the problem of unemployment.

Decrease in Cottage Industries

Industrialisation has created closure of cottage industries. As a result cottage industries have met an end. Machine made goods are good and attractive. They are also sold at less price. These factors have contributed to decrease in cottage industries.

Capitalist-Labour Conflict

Industrialisation has brought capitalist and labourers in conflict. Capitalists are accused as exploiter and oppressors by labourers. Labour unionism has emerged in public sector. Unionism leads to indiscipline in work organisation. This hampers the production and functioning of an industry. Strike and locking also take place. As a result some industries are declared as sick.

Gap between Rich and Poor

Industrialisation has created a big gap between rich and poor. The capitalist leads luxurious life with all modern facilities. A good number of people lead life below poverty line. In order to maintain existence, they do beggary and immoral acts. It is because morality is not a binding force for poor who struggle hard for survival.

Progress in Transportation and Communication

Due to industrialisation, progress in transportation and communication has taken place. Today we have railway, buses, aeroplane, ship, telephone, computer, internet and cell phones.

These means of transportation and communication are found in industrial urban areas.

Complex Division of Labour

Industrialisation has created complex division of labour. Here, division of labour is not based on age and sex. Here division of labour is based on expertise and specialisation.

9
Institutions of Complex Society

Like simple society, the smallest unit of complex society is also family. Family is also primary institution in complex society. Through family, needs of family members are fulfilled. In simple society lineage, clan and caste groups reside together in different areas of villages. In urban area lineage, clan and caste are not a corporeal kin groups. It is because all members do not live in one town, they live in several towns. Some of them also live in villages. In urban society, inter-caste and inter-religious marriages are taking place. Here clan and caste had become functionless. Here, a couple belongs to different caste groups and religious groups. Siblings belong to different lineage and caste groups. They trace lineage relation from father and mother side. Clan group is not so strong as in simple society.

In complex society, there are municipality, municipal corporation, notified area, cantonment area and urban area like institutions.

In complex society, an individual is not combined only to his relatives, but also related to a number of secondary groups. His social net is up to occupational groups, friend groups, linguistic groups, regional groups, national groups and international groups. He/she is also related to Governmental institutions and Non-Governmental institutions. The social network of an individual in complex society is very complex.

The complex society has plural culture and religion. People of different communities reside together and practice their own religions, faiths and visit their places of worship.

Thus, institutions of complex society are as follows:

- Family in Complex Society
- Kinship in Complex Society

- Religion in Complex Society
- Administrative Institutions in Complex Society
- Social Network in Complex Society.

Now let us discuss about these institutions one by one.

Family in Complex Society

Family occupies an important place in complex society as a basic infrastructural institution of man. It influences both individual and society in different ways. Towns and villages are two centres of different cultures. The culture of both these places differ profoundly. The village institutions have a long history of past. But a town is a product of urbanisation and industrialisation. Thick population, different occupations, different business, trade, commerce, specialisation of labour, industrial production, mechanical civilization and culture are symbols of urban life. Urban style of life, impersonal relation, formality, artificiality, expectancy and slums are closely related to urban life. These all factors have provided a special form to urban family. Urban family differs from rural family. Urbanisation and industrialisation has made a great change in urban family. One does not find the concept of joint family. It has created only nuclear family which includes husband, wife and unmarried children. It has also created single parent family.

Characteristics of Family in Complex Society

We can discuss the characteristics of family in complex society under the following sub-headings:

Individualistic Approach

The urban family is characterised by individualistic approach of family members. Here every individual member is owner of his/her own will. He/she does whatever he/she likes to do. No other family member comes in between him/her and his/her desire. He/she does not have words like good and bad, *pap* and *punya, Swarga* and *Naraka,* moral and immoral. He/she can use any medium to get his/her desire fulfilled. He/she does not have pressure, control and abstraction. He/she lives in own erected house and dies in the same erected house.

Selfish Family

The nature of urban family is selfish. Urban family has relation with only those family from whom its desire is fulfilled or expected to be fulfilled. As soon as desire is fulfilled, relationship is broken. Here, relation with other family is not permanent. It is transitory. Interest and desire creates relationship or destroys relationship in urban family.

Small Size

The size of urban family is small. It includes husband, wife and one or two unmarried children.

Nuclear Family

The structure of urban family is not joint, rather its structure is nuclear which has husband, wife and one or two unmarried children.

Single Parent Family

In urban society, one finds the existence of single parent family. This is happening due to high incidence in divorce or sudden death of husband or wife.

Semi-broken Family

In urban family, a good number comes from those families, whose either husband or wife works in another towns. Children reside either with father or with mother. The number of semi-broken families is more in urban society.

Equal Status of Women

In urban family, both husband and wife enjoy equal status. She is not only wife but friend, life partner and adviser of husband. She plays significant role in family level decision-making such as education of children, marketing, erecting house, marriage of children, maintaining of relationship and exchanging gifts and presents with relatives, friends and neighbours. Husband is dependent on wife for family level decision. Girls are also free to get education either from house or from hostels. Generally, urban girls prefer to live in hostel/lodge to accomplish the education of U.G./P.G. Law, engineering, medical, management, administration, technical education and others. They are getting employment as engineers, doctor, lawyer, professor, I.T. engineers, managers and administrators. The marriage in urban family has become individual work of family. Boys and girls select partners from own choice. Thus, in urban family both boys and girls, and husband and wife enjoy equal status.

Imbalance in Family Relation

In urban industrial family father is not a controlling authority. There, father/mother and children all are individualistic. They have individual approach regarding life, education, career, marriage, festivals and ceremonies. They do not accept control of any person in their individual life and decision. All members enjoy freedom in decision-making. The feeling of too much independence has created some imbalances in family relation.

Downfall of Family Occupation

Urban family does not want to engage their children in their own family occupation. They want to provide them good education so that they could do good jobs or run good business. They never want to involve them in own traditional occupation. As a result, downfall of family occupation is taking place in urban family.

Increase in Divorce

In urban family, wives are educated and working. They have independent earning. They enjoy equality and freedom. But the feeling of equality and freedom become the cause of divorce in urban family. It is because they do not want to make compromise. They do not like to bear exploitation and oppression even at psychological level. They are now powerful and raise voices for their rights. They move to the court against exploitation, oppression, deprivation and violation. They seek divorce gladly and become ready to bear the burden of rearing and educating children. This has increased the incidence of divorce in urban family.

Decrease in Religiosity and Spirituality

In urban family, one does not get the value of religion and spiritualism. Here religion and spirituality are taken as symbols of backwardness. Here, every member is progressive and has scientific and practical approach. Members never talk about *Pap-Punya, Dharma-Adharma, Swarga-Naraka, Sukarma-Dushkarma, Naitik-Anaitik, Punar Janma-Moksha*. They treat this earth as heaven and money as *moksha*. Thus, in urban family one finds decrease in religiosity and spirituality.

Formal and Showy Behaviour

The behaviour of members in urban industrial society is formal and showy. This does not include naturality. Their all behaviour from morning to evening are full of formality and artificiality. Saying good morning in the morning, saying good day in day time, saying good noon at noon time, saying good evening in evening and saying good night at night are not our natural behaviour. Similarly, saying thank you for doing any work is also not our natural behaviour. Calling mother as Mama and Father as Dad is also artificial behaviour. Similarly, hello, hi, ok are also artificial behaviour. Thus, in urban family members behave artificially not naturally. Sharing food on dining table, sitting on sofa, sleeping in bed, having A.C., T.V., Scooter, motor cycle and car are all for show.

Some New Trends of Urban Family

The family of cities and metropolises is undergoing fast changes. As a result of fast changes, following recent trends have emerged in urban and metropolitan society:

The Work of Family by Other Institutions

In urban and metropolitan society, a good number of such institutions have emerged which are performing functions of family. For example, hotel, restaurant, industry, children rearing home, oldage care home, nursing homes, play schools and others. There are a number of families where food is not cooked for several days in house. Members visit restaurants or have online delivery of desired food. It is because all members are working. They feel tired after performing jobs. They do not want to cook. Working husband and wife have *Aaya* to look after and rear their children. They also give their children to child caring centres and play schools. Previously pickles and *papad* were made in house but now they are produced by factories. Parents are being sent in old age home where their oldhood is looked after by paid employees of the institution. Children are also being sent to hostels, play schools or nursing schools. The couple feel proud in observing such behaviour. They say openly that their parents had sent them in hostels during childhood and we have sent them in old age home.

Decrease in Sex Morality

There has been decrease in sex morality in urban and metropolitan family. This has increased the incidence of pre-marital and extra-marital relationship. For them sex is not related to religious and moral values. It is a thing and needs to be satisfied by any one at any time. It does not become impure by pre-marital or extra-marital relations. Sex industries and contraceptives are promoting such behaviour. The couple wants to satisfy sex but does not want to produce children. They want to adopt children. Some prefer to live in relationship as husband and wife without marriage. Sex rackets and call girls occupation are on increase in cities and metropolises. All such practices show sufficient light on decrease of sex morality in urban family.

Equality between Husband and Wife

In urban family husband and wife are enjoying equal status. The feeling of equality has made both husband and wife to think freely and behave freely. Both know what is proper-improper, good-bad, advantageous-disadvantageous, theoretical-practical, right-wrong etc.

Small Family Size

The family size of urban and metropolitan society has become very small. The couple does not like to produce more than one or two children. Some couple does not like to produce even a single child. In place of producing a child, they adopt a child from surrogate mother. Some couple does not enter into marital relation but live in relationship as husband and wife without marriage. There are a good number of family having single child or no child. Here couple like to lead a lavish life and have a good bank balance.

Compromise between Husband and Wife

In urban and cosmopolitan society, the relation between husband and wife is not based on religious value, it is based on compromise. This compromise can be broken any time for any cause. This has destabilised the family life.

Centre of Entertainment

Today the family of urban and metropolitan society has become a centre of indoor entertainment. Colour T.V., V.C.P., V.C.R. Computer, Cell phones internet-services all have become a means of entertainment. Family members make entertainment inside house.

Political Awareness

The family of urban and metropolitan city remains politically conscious. All members—husband, wife and children have free political discussions on regional, national and international politics. Family members may be supporters of one political parties or of different political parties. At the time of breakfast and sharing meals, members have political discussion.

Causes of Destability and Disorganisation of Urban Family

It is true that urban family is facing the problem of destability and disorganisation in urban and metropolitan society. We can discuss the causes of destability and disorganistion in urban and metropolitan family under following sub-headings:

Love Marriage and Inter-caste Marriage

The western civilization and culture of complex society is encouraging inter-caste and love marriage. In this type of marriage aspiration of couple occupies significant place. Such marriages are based on compromise, not on religious and moral value. Here a wife does not consider herself as *Ardhangani* and her husband as lord. They do not believe in husband-wife relation for seven generations. They treat each other as friend, life partner and co-workers. They do not consider the practical aspect of marriage. Whenever they face any problem, they break compromise and seek divorce. As a result, the cases of single parent is increasing in urban and metropolitan family.

Working Woman-related Problem

In urban and metropolitan family wives are working. Being working, they have to adjust themselves with duty hours and daily going and coming back from office. The structure of family is nuclear, which includes husband, wife and one or two unmarried children. Working women have to perform duty in offices as well as in houses. Performing duties at two places result in negligence of children and husband-wife conflict. This is not a healthy situation for family life. But urban and metropolitan family is facing such problem. It is because, performing duties in home and office requires adjustment and cooperation of husband and children.

Problem of Sexual Adjustment

In urban and metropolitan families, husband and wife face the problem of sexual adjustment. A tired working woman is not an object. It cannot be expected from her that she should fulfil the sexual desire of husband regularly. She is also a living being. She is not an object to be used if and when one desires. Due to bodily tiredness and office workload on working woman, the sexual desire of husband is not fulfilled satisfactorily. In this situation, a husband becomes drunkard and develops extra-marital relation.

Lack of Adjustment in Ideas

The family members of complex society have their own free ideas. Husband, wife and children possess different ideas. The difference in ideas and thinking creates problem related to ideological adjustment. Lack of ideological adjustment sometimes causes disintegration of urban and metropolitan families.

Individualistic Nature of Members

In urban and metropolitan families members are of individualistic nature. Each member thinks for his/her own progress. Husband and wife are working. Both remain busy in own duty and promotion. Children remain busy in education and career. No member thinks for other members of family. They remain together externally but remain separated internally. No member cares for food and health of other members. All such situations ultimately lead towards disintegration of family.

Lack of Discipline

The family of urban and cosmopolitan society lacks discipline. Husband and wife share wine together, visit separate club, perform dance with own friends, visit restaurants with friends, go to cinema and mall with friend. Children also visit cinema, mall, zoo, museum, picnic, planetorium and other places with own friends. Thus, family of complex society lacks couple discipline. This behaviour ultimately leads towards disintegration.

Not Sharing Responsibility

Family members of urban and metropolitan family do not want to share social responsibility. Late marriage has become a fashion. Remaining unmarried or living in relation has become a fashion. After marriage couple does not prefer to produce a child. They prefer to adopt a child from surrogate mother. If they produce a child, they do not pay proper attention. They have *Aaya* to take care of child or send to hostel or nursery school. They do not have emotional feeling and attachment. The children on becoming young and adult are sending their old parents to old age home.

Lack of Security

Family of urban and metropolitan society lack feeling of security. There is no joint family, lineage, clan, caste like villages to provide security during troubles. Being of individualistic nature, each member lacks emotional security, husband, wife and children do not feel secure. There is no one to settle dispute between husband and wife and between children. This leads to individual disorganisation.

Future of Family in Complex Society

There is no doubt that family of complex society is facing a number of problems. Here a family is totally influenced by Western culture and civilization. Such situations are arising day after day that is why a family is bound to disintegrate. Families have become individualistic and competitive for adopting and leading artificial life. All family members are working to achieve means of living lavishly. They are taking over-time duty. They have become machine. They get up, go to washroom, have tea and breakfast, go to office, have lunch, come back home or spend night in office. Seeing and caring old parents and children are taken as great burden. Children are sent in Shishu Sewa Sadan, play schools and hostels. Old Parents are sent in oldage home or Vridhdha Sewa Sadan. Working couples are sharing food not by self-cooking but in hotels and restaurants. Young boy and girl have started living in relation without marriage. They fulfil their biological needs by living in relation, but not satisfying their social needs by producing children. A number of institutions have emerged which are involved in performing functions of a family. In this situation of change, people have started thinking about the future of family in complex society. Will this institution vanish or maintain its existence in future.

It is true that a number of couples are running away from the responsibility of producing children. A number of young boy and girl do not want to lead a married life. They prefer to live in relation. Today, persons of same sex, i.e. male-male and female-female are arranging marriages. It is also true that family of complex society is facing the situation of destabilisation and desintegration. But this cannot be concluded that marriage and family will come to end in complex society. In fact, marriage and family perform some such important and unsecondary functions, which cannot be performed by other institutions. These significant and non-secondary functions are as follows:

- Permanent sex satisfaction
- Lineage system
- Legal children
- Emotional attachment
- Permanent feeling of security
- Permanent life partner.

Due to above significant and non-secondary functions, the existence of marriage and family will always be maintained in complex society. This institution will never vanish.

Kinship System in Complex Society

Kinship is a model of relationship based on parentage and marriage. Thus, it includes such groups which are formed on the basis of blood relation and marriage relation. Siblings, cousins, lineage and clans are groups based on blood relation. They are consanguineal kins. But relations formed after marriage of a person are called affinal kins.

In simple society, an individual is dependent on kinship right from birth to death. Here family, lineage and clan reside together. Relatives formed on the basis of marriage are found living in neighbouring villages. During trouble, consanguineal kins and affinal kins come together to solve the problem.

The complex society is not based on kinship. Here an individual lives in nuclear family. Here, he/she lives far away from his/her lineage clan group members. Here, siblings, lineage, clan and caste groups are not in the form of neighbour. Here, neighbour belongs to other caste, lineage, clan and religion. Thus, siblings, lineage and clan, and caste group are not corporeal kin groups here. Here families of different caste and religion reside together.

In simple society, marriage takes place following caste endogamy and clan exogamy rules. Love and inter-caste marriages are not allowed. But in complex society, inter-caste, inter-religious marriages are occurring. Even within caste intra-clan marriages are taking place. Here a couple is not necessary of same caste, different clan and same religion. Here, kinship bondage is free from caste, clan and religious bondage.

Characteristics of Kinship System in Complex Society

We can discuss the characteristics of kinship system of complex society under following sub-headings:

Inter-clan Couple

In complex society, the clan system has lost its value. Clan exogamy rule is being violated. As a result, intra-clan couples have come into existence in urban and metropolitan city.

Inter-Caste Couple

In complex society, the caste endogamy rule of marriage has become valueless. In place of intra-caste marriage, inter-caste marriages are taking place frequently. As a result of such practice, inter-caste couples have come into existence in complex society.

Inter-Religious Couple

In complex society, not only inter-caste marriages are taking place, but inter-religious marriages are also occurring. This practice has created inter-religious couple.

Nuclear Family

In complex society, there is existence of nuclear family which includes husband, wife and their unmarried one or two children.

Double Descent

The siblings of inter-caste and inter-religious couple trace their descent both from father side and mother side.

Neo-local Family

In complex society, the couple and their children reside in self-erected new house. Thus, the family is neo-local.

Non-corporeal Kin Groups

In complex society, siblings, lineage and clan like corporeal kin groups are not found. They are located at far distant places. They do not function as corporeal kin groups.

Lack of Emotional Attachment

Kin groups lack emotional attachment because they have become individualistic and competitive. They have artificial relation, not emotional relation.

Formal Relation

Different affinal and consanguineal kins maintain formal relations. They show formality on birth, marriage and death ceremonies. They come for few hours with an arrangement to return.

Regional Expansion of Kin Groups

In complex society, consanguineal and affinal kin groups have regional expansion.

National Expansion of Kin Groups

In complex society, kin groups have national expansion. They are spread in different towns, cities and metropolises

International Expansion of Kin Groups

In complex society, kin groups also have international expansion because some of them are spread in different foreign countries.

Conflict between Kins

In complex society, conflicting relations are found between different kins due to division of paternal properties.

Religion in Complex Society

In complex society, people belonging to different religious faith reside together as a community. They practice their own religious beliefs. They have their own religious symbols where they go to offer worship and prayer. They have their own religious specialists and religious festivals. Thus, in complex society one finds the existence of different religious symbols, rituals, beliefs, traditions, festivals and specialists. The theoretical aspect of religion is seen in complex society. Here specialists of different religions come to preach the people of community about the importance of religion and achievement in following values of religion. They analyse religious values on the basis of sacred texts. Religious scholars and thinkers make analysis of different aspects of religion.

In complex society, both atheist and non-atheist reside together. Here some people remain busy in worship of his/her God and deity. Some people are such who consider welfare of human society as their *Dharma*. Thus, in complex society, two forms of *Dharma* appear. The thinkers of the one group treat the welfare of entire world as their *Dharma*. Such thinkers do not have own caste, community, region and nation. The welfare of human beings of world community is their *Dharma*. On the other hand, majority of people are such who perform religious activities keeping their interests in mind. We can call it as individual *Dharma*. The religion of complex society is individualistic. An individual is free to accept or reject religion. He/she can change his religion. He/she is free to praise or criticise religion. That is why in complex society secularisation of religion has its own significance.

Complex society has been centre of religious movement. Here, a number of religious theories have been propounded. A number of blind faith have been discarded. Arya Samaj, Brahmo

Samaj, Prarthna Samaj, Ramkrishna Mission are product of these urban religious movements.

Characteristics of Urban Religion

We can discuss the characteristics of urban religion under following sub-headings:

Individual Religion

One of the characteristics of urban religion is individual. It may be termed as individual religion. Whether an individual worships or not, it is completely his/her own matter. Again an individual offers worship to Gods and Goddesses by any method is also his/her individual affair. He/she will perform life cycle rituals by which method or he/she will not perform life cycle rituals, it is also his/her affair. Thus, an individual is completely free to perform rituals and worships, celebrate festivals and visit to religious symbols or not. Nobody can force him/her for religious performance. It depends completely on his/her will.

Lack of Collective Sentiment

Due to individualistic nature of religion in complex society, the religion lacks collective sentiment. Here *Puja-Path, Bhajan, Kirtan* are not done keeping collective sentiment in mind. Here *Puja Path, Bhajan, Kirtan* and rituals are performed keeping individual interest in mind. For wish fulfilment and after wish fulfilment, he/she performs worship, visit to temples and pilgrimage centre. Worship is not done by the individual for welfare of entire community.

Lack of Collective Participation

The religion of complex society being individualistic does not show collective participation. On some special occasions, individual becomes participant of collective worship. For example, *Yagya* and religious procession of Durga Puja, Ramnavami, Rath Yatra and others. Contrary to this, in Islam and Christianity, there is collective participation. For example, *Namaz* of *Jumma* is offered collectively. On the occasion of *Eid* and *Bakarid* collective *Namaz* is offered. Christians also offer prayer collectively. But such occasions cannot be connected to daily religious activities.

Leaving some special occasions, members of complex society do not offer collective worship.

Changing Nature of Theoretical and Practical Aspects

The theoretical and practical aspects of religion in complex society are not static, rather they are changing. The complex society is a centre of scientific achievements and consciousness. Here, people have logical and scientific approach. Materialistic culture and civilisation has made people more aware and logical. Therefore, an individual does not accept the theory of religion by closing eyes. That is why the religion of complex society is found changing.

Short Time Performance

The complex society does not have time, money and patience for long time ritual performances. Individual wants to complete religious performances in very short time. That is why he makes summarisation of rituals and sacred performances. For example, the rituals of marriage which take many days are now performed in few hours. Death rituals are also performed in three-four days instead of 13 days. Now, individual does not want to spend more time and money unnecessary in the name of religion and religious performances.

Importance of Decoration in Religious Performances

In the religion of complex society, special attention is paid on the decoration of the place. Here individuals have become competitive in show and decoration. Pandals are decorated in special design for Durga Puja, religious preaches, *Yagya* and *Hawana*. Electric decorations are made. Modern music and songs are played. Modern dances are performed. Media makes the people know about such religious performances so that people could gather in a great crowd. Tickets are also sold for modern dances. Thus, one finds more pomp and show and decoration in religious performance of complex society.

Lack in Emotional Commitment

In religion of complex society, one finds lack of emotional commitment. Members of complex society participate in religious performances as formality to show their presence to organisers. But they do not participate whole-heartedly. They come because they are invited. They never come, if they do not get invitation.

Secularisation

Each religion of complex society observes secularism. Followers of each religion perform rituals, observe traditions, and do religious activities as per own religious values and faiths. They do not see religious values and faiths of other religion inferior or superior. In religious processions they help each other.

Lack in Fanaticism

In complex society, one finds existence of less fanaticism. Here people are progressive and logical. They are broad hearted not narrow minded. Urbanisation, industrialisation and scientific progress have changed the outlook of people completely. Here people of different religion work together in office, hostel, restaurants, cinema hall, mall, railway station, bus stand and industry. They share meal together. People of different religion meet shoulder to shoulder on religious occasion and offer congratulation. In this way, one finds less fanaticism in complex society.

Administration in Complex Society

In order to maintain administrative system in complex society, there are institutions like Municipality, Municipal Corporation. Notified area committee and cantonment board. Through these urban administrative system, administration is maintained in complex society. Now let us discuss about these urban administration one by one.

Municipality

In small town municipality is established. For establishment of municipality, there are following conditions:

- The population of a town should not be less than 5,000.
- The density of population should be 1000 per sq. mile.
- 75 per cent of total population should have non-agricultural occupation.

The municipality is established by State Government. The municipality has following parts:

- Municipality council

- Chairman and Deputy Chairman
- Committees.

Each municipality has a municipality council whose members are known as councillors. This council has minimum 10 members and maximum 40 members. The number of members is decided on the basis of population of the town. 4/5 part of members are elected and 1/5 part of members are nominated. The period of municipality council is of 5 years. This can be dissolved even before completion of terms. For the purpose of election, a town is divided into several wards. Number of persons to be elected from each ward is decided on the basis of population of a ward. This is an institution where exchange of ideas related to town is made among councillors. The meeting of councillors takes place once in a month. Special meeting is organised on the basis of written petition of the councillor.

All members of municipality committee elect one member as Chairman and one other member as Deputy Chairman. These posts are honorary for five years. The Chairman and Deputy Chairman can be removed from the posts by 2/3rd majority. They can be removed, if they do not obey the order of Government. The Chairman looks after daily work of municipality. He/she executes the decision taken by the council.

Different committees are constituted to look after the daily work of the municipality. For example, education committee, finance committee, and health and sanitation committee.

The chairperson chairs the meeting of different committees.

Work of Municipality

The work of municipality can be divided into two forms:

- Essential work
- Optional work.

Essential Work

The essential works of municipality are as follows:

- Sanitation system of town
- Construction and repair of roads
- Electricity and lighting arrangement
- Drinking water

- Cleanliness of public places
- Drainage system
- Primary education
- Public market
- Hospital
- Cremation and burial places
- Meat shops
- Birth and Death Record
- Control of Fire.

Optional Work

The optional works of municipality are as follows:

- Construction of new road and drainage
- To make dirty places livable
- Erection of new building
- House for poor
- Arrangement of milk
- Control of flood
- Transport arrangement
- Exhibition of different kinds
- Development of parks
- Development of museum
- To abandon very old buildings.

Source of Income

The sources of income of municipality are as follows:

- Collection of taxes from houses
- Collection of taxes from markets
- Water tax
- Garbage tax
- Lighting tax
- Occupation tax
- Education tax
- Lavatory tax
- Governmental grants
- Governmental loan.

Municipal Corporation

In big city, there is administrative system of Nagar Nigam or Municipal Corporation. There are three important parts of municipal corporation. They are as follows:

- Corporation council
- Permanent committee
- Chief Administrative Officer.

The number of members of municipal corporation is decided on the basis of population of town. In the corporation council, there are elected members, representative member, nominated member and official members. The municipal corporation work as an assembly for policy decision regarding the development of city. Two types of meeting are held in council of members—common meeting and special meeting. Common meeting is held once in a month, but special meeting is held to take decision on special issue. Previously, Mayor and Deputy Mayor were elected in the very first meeting of councillors. But now-a-days, they are selected directly by voters. The post of Mayor and Deputy Mayor is honorary, but now-a-days payment is made. Mayor conducts the meeting of the municipal council. In his absence, Deputy Mayor conducts the meeting. He/she does not perform any administrative work. He/she is first citizen of the city. In this way, he/she holds significant place in urban and metropolitan society.

The second important part of municipal corporation is permanent committee. It has members according to the number of ward councillors. Permanent Committee conducts work related to ruling in municipal corporation. Mayor and Deputy Mayor are also its member. Chief administrative officer has to seek approval of this committee for implementing any decision. Its meeting is held once in a month.

The chief administrative officer is appointed by the Government. He/she belongs to I.A.S. Cadre. He/she functions according to rules related to the functioning of municipal corporation. He/she implements the rules of municipal corporation.

Main Functions of Municipal Corporation

- To construct drainage

- To construct common lavatory
- Water supply and lighting
- Garbage management
- Cremation ground and burial ground
- Birth and death census
- Birth and death certificates
- Arrangement of vaccination
- To prevent expansion of infectious diseases
- Construction of common hospitals
- Arrangement of veterinary services
- Construction of welfare buildings
- Road, bridge construction
- Primary schools, library and reading room construction
- Common park, garden, tank, ghat, exercise room construction
- Control of fire
- Transport arrangement
- Exhibition and fair arrangement
- Market and meat shop arrangement.

Besides above work, corporation can do any type of work which is related to the interest and benefit of the people. It disposes every type of work from birth to death of a city-dweller.

Besides Chief Administration Officer, the corporation has Deputy Administrative Officer, City Engineer, Health Officer, Town Planner and Security Officer.

The source of income of corporation is tax, grant, fees, cash punishment and loan. Corporation can impose taxes on house, water, light, holding, lavatory, occupation, transport, rickshaw, auto, market, ghat etc.

Mega Municipal Corporation

Now-a-days, metropolitan cities have mega municipal corporation. They have big population and more number of wards and councillors. The functioning style of mega municipal corporation is more or less same as that of municipal corporation.

Cantonment Board

Towns which have army cantonment area, are controlled by

cantonment board. The cantonment board administration is separate from municipality, municipal corporation and mega municipal corporation. On cantonment area, Department of Defence, Government of India has control over it through the medium of Cantonment Board. Its some members are elected and some members are nominated by Government of India.

Port Trust

Towns and cities having sea ports, are controlled by Port Trust. Its some members are elected and some members are nominated by the Government. Its main function is to maintain health, sanitation, lighting and stay arrangement of visitors. Its source of income is limited to tax and Government aid.

Notified Area

The town which has a population of more than 10,000 and less than 20,000, there Government forms a Notified Area Committee to look after the administration of the town. It has 5 to 7 members. It is known as semi-municipal corporation. Its some members are elected and some members are nominated by the Government. The main source of income of this committee is limited tax and Government grant.

Social Network of Complex Society

In complex society, an individual is not limited only to family members and relatives. He/she is related to members of occupational group, commercial group, service group, club members, friend's society, voluntary organisation, non-governmental organisations, welfare society and peace committee and others. Thus, his/her network areas are very big. He/she is related to members of family and neighbourhood to regional, national and international community.

In complex society, more relatedness of an individual to more number of institutions reflect his/her expansion of social network. All individuals do not have expansion of network at town, region, national and international level. But there are some individuals who are nationally and internationally renowned, have expansion of social network spread at national and international level. Some individuals have very limited expansion of network related to family, neighbour and relatives. Opposite to it, some persons are related to a number of organisations which have regional, national and international spread. The expansion of network of such persons is not only local but global level. In complex society, a person is related to a number of secondary groups. Therefore, he/she has large area of network coverage.

In rural society, the expansion of social network is limited to family, lineage, clan, caste, village, relatives of neighbouring villages and neighbouring market and health centres and neighbouring towns. But in complex society, network of a person is very expansive which have regional, national and international spread.

In complex society, an individual has following social network:

- Network with own villages
- Network with villages of relatives
- Network with relatives living in same town
- Network with relatives living in different towns in India
- Network with relatives living in foreign countries
- Network with friends living in own town, different towns, own country and in foreign countries.
- Departmental network with working fellow and officers
- Network with neighbourhood
- Network with shopkeepers
- Network with doctors
- Network with administrators
- Network with politicians
- Network with police officers
- Network with entertainment club
- Network with Peace Committee
- Trade network at town, regional, national and international level
- Network with welfare society
- Network with voluntary organisation
- Network with NGOs
- Network with caste society
- Network with linguistic society
- Network with unions
- Network with contractors

- Network with entrepreneurs
- Network with enterprisers
- Network with scholars
- Network with social worker
- Network with religious preacher
- Network with salon and beauty parlour
- Network with schools, colleges and universities
- Network with artists and painters
- Network with architect
- Network with engineer
- Network with Administrative Officers
- Network with Ministers.

10
Urban Planning

The meaning of town planning is to formulate plans for facing different types of known and unknown urban problems. Plans are formulated for future course of action. Its purpose is to explore problems and formulate policies and programme for their impletation. Its purpose is to provide maximum facility to town-dwellers and to beautify the town. Through town planning the interest of town-dwellers are protected. Thus, town planning is a special type of approach which is directly related to the development of town and to provide amenities to town-dwellers.

In our country, programmes of urban development have been formulated and implemented since our Independence. Right from 1st Five Year Plan to 12th Five Year Plan of Planning Commission and present NITI Ayog, Government of India, special attention has been given on town planning for the development of towns. Our country has a number of towns. Some are religious, some are historical, some are commercial and some are industrial. All towns do not have equal problems. The size of each town is also not equal. Therefore, the form of town planning for each town is also not similar.

Due to industrial growth in our country, rise in urban population has taken place. Today nearly 30 per cent people reside in towns whereas 70 per cent people are still village-dwellers. The density of population in town is increasing. The towns are facing population pressure. Mills, factories, industries, markets are being established in nearby towns. They are creating a number of problems related to towns. They have become challenge for the development of towns. Town-dwellers are facing problems of house, water, electricity, food supply, slums and a number of health related problems. They are also facing social pathological problems like poverty, unemployment, juvenile delinquency, and intoxication. They are also facing the problem of lack of parks and entertainment centres. Proper roads, drainage and transport facilities are not provided to town-dwellers. Such problems have made the life of urban-dwellers hell-like. The problem of air, water, sound and food pollution is creating a number of serious and non-curable diseases. In order to solve these problems, town planning is very important. Town planning is made keeping town problems in mind on one hand, and to provide different facilities to town-dwellers on the other hand. The reconstruction of towns is main part of town planning. Good transport system, good electric supply, good hospitals, good schools, colleges, universities, law colleges, law universities, technical and management institutes, road, drainage, houses, means of entertainment, play ground, slums development, sanitation in *Jhuggi-Jhopari,* cremation ground, burial ground and good communication etc. are different areas of town planning. In summary, we can say that through town planning different problems are solved and physical structure is prepared in such a way so that hygienic environment could be maintained.

Now-a-days, town planning has become an important aspect of NITI Aayog. Attempts are being made to solve problems of towns and make a beautiful and attractive look to towns.

Basic Elements of Urban Planning

We can discuss the basic elements of town planning under following sub-headings:

Control of Traffic System

Town and metropolis dwellers have to face problems of transport. Narrow, small, up-down pits on road, people do not move easily, what to say about vehicles. People face the problem of road jams frequently. Town planning decides the minimum width of a street and road. New roads and streets are built. Roads are made wide. New traffic system is established. By-pass roads, flyover, big and small bridges are constructed. Pedestrian street and crossing over are made. Taxi stand, car stand, auto stand and bus stand are established. Traffic rules are implemented. Electric supply, water supply and communication system are established. Attempts are made for waterways, roadways and airways. Visitors, passengers and traders are given maximum facilities to avail. Traffic police post is established to control the vehicles running on roads. Traffic signals are displayed at traffic posts and are followed by vehicle drivers. Thus, control of traffic system is a basic element of town planning.

Control of Use of Land

The encroachment of land is also a basic problem related to towns and cities. People encroach public barren land, road, street, park, garden, drain, *chauk,* bus stand, railway station and other places. To make town and cities free from encroachment is also a work of town planning. Town planner decides length and breadth of road, street and drainage. It also decides length, breadth and height of multi-storeied building, market complex, malls, cinema halls and other buildings. The town planning decides the rule of map construction of house, building, multi-storey complex, market complex and other construction work. The maps need to be approved by Nagar Nigam or Mega Nagar Nigam.

Construction of Houses for Different Classes

In town and cities people of lower income group, middle income group and high income group reside. Town planning emphasises upon residences of different classes, construction of houses or allotment of land plots, construction of hostels for students, working women etc. Colonies for officials and other Government servants are made according to plan.

Reconstruction of Slums

Reconstruction of slums and providing amenities to slum-dwellers is also one of works of town planning. Their houses are reconstructed. Electricity and water connections are provided. Lavatories are made. Health and sanitation facilities are given.

Facility of Park and Common Places

Creation, development, beautification and protection of common places and parks are taken up by town planning.

Electricity and Water Supply

Electricity and water supply are very important for town planning. Town planning emphasises upon regular supply of electricity and water in private and public houses, offices, institutes, markets, malls, multi-storeied flats, parks, bus stand and other common places. The supply of water is a problem at one hand and to supply pollution-free water is a problem on the other hand. Therefore, town planning emphasises on supply of pure water and regular electricity for the development of towns and town-dwellers.

Garbage Management

Garbage management is an important task of town planning. Everyday hundreds tonnes of garbage comes on road, drainage, houses, malls, multi-storey buildings, market centres, hotels and restaurants. To provide proper management to garbage disposal is an important item of town planning. It is because without proper garbage management, the life of city-dwellers will become hell. The town planning makes special attention on sewage system and disposal of garbage.

Parking Place

In towns we find vehicles of various types like cycle, rikshaw, auto-rikshaw, taxi, car, minibus and bus. There is urgent need for a proper parking system for different types of vehicles. To decide, develop and protect parking places occupies significant place in town planning.

Zonal System

To divide towns into different zones for development purpose is an important element of town planning. For example, commercial and trade zone, official zone, industrial zone, residential zone. common entertainment zone and others. Division of town into different zones is essential from the point of new of traffic and crowd control.

Development of Neighbourhood Feeling

In town an individual becomes impersonal. He/she lives in common multi-storey building but does not know his/her neighbour. Therefore, an important task of town planning is to create we-feeling among neighbours. For this purpose, colony or residential complex with park facilities are created so that people could meet with each other on Sunday and other holidays. And a we-feeling could develop among them.

Problems Related to Urban Planning

Town planning has to face a number of problems. The problems of town planning can be discussed under following sub-headings:

- Rapidly increasing population
- Land encroachment
- Garbage management
- New slums
- Influential individual
- Lack of discipline
- Theft of water and electricity
- Shifting of *khatals*
- Shifting of Jhuggi-Jhopari
- Corruption.

Now let us discuss about these causes one by one :

Rapidly Increasing Population

The population of urban and metropolitan cities is increasing very rapidly. The fast increase in population is creating not only problem of housing, but also unemployment, slums, *Jhuggi-Jhopari* and other social pathological problems. The increase in population become more than expectation of the planner.

Land Encroachment

Land encroachment has also become a major problem in town planning. People have encroached government lands for house, shop, stall, slum and *Jhuggi-Jhopari*. The rate of land encroachment is also very fast. It creates a problem in planning of town. Land encroachment is creating difficulties in achieving the goal of town and city development.

Garbage Problem

In towns and metropolitan cities lakhs and lakhs people come daily by different modes of transport and communication. They do their work and return their homes. Such a huge number of daily goers and comers deposit tonnes and tonnes of garbage here and there. This creates a great problem in maintaining sanitation of cities and metropolises. Thus, garbage management problem comes in the way of proper implementation of town planning.

Emergence of New Slums

The population of cities and metropolises increasing day by day. As a result new slums are emerging besides the old slums. It is creating a problem in maintaining town planning.

Influential Individuals

In cities and metropolises, there are some individuals who have approach and connection to politicians and, police and administrators. They may be politicians/elites and other influential personalities. They hold important positions in the society. They are also involved in land encroachment. They move to court and delay the development of town. Due to their influence town planning is not achieving its target in renovating slums, removing *Jhuggi-Jhopari, Khatal,* shops, *thela* and widening of road and road construction.

Lack of Discipline

Lack of discipline in town and city-dwellers is also coming in the way to maintain the town planning and its target. Digging road, breaking road, encroaching road, making road dirty, defecation in drains, urinating at public place, spitting after chewing betels, throwing garbage here and there, using plastic and throwing on road and throwing banana cover on road are included in daily activities of city-dwellers from morning till late night. Thus, lack of discipline is creating hindrance in achieving the target of town planning.

Theft of Water and Electricity

Some town and city-dwellers make theft of electricity and water. As a result other town and city-dwellers do not get regular supply of water and electricity. Regular bill payers have to face a great problem for electricity and water. Thus, theft of water and electricity creates hindrance in maintaining the town planning.

Shifting of Khatals

Shifting of *khatals* also creates problem in maintaining the aim of town planning. Whenever the administration wants to remove *khatal* away from town and city, movements arises. Many elites and politicians come to support them. They move to the court and delay the shifting of *khatals*.

Shifting of Jhuggi-Jhopari

Shifting of *Jhuggi-Jhopari* is also coming in the way of maintaining the aim of town planning. Here also some politicians come to organise movement for restoring the *Jhuggi-Jhopari*. They stop the shifting work of *Jhuggi-Jhopari*.

Anthropological Approaches to Urban Planning

Anthropologists emphasise more on human, social and cultural aspects of town planning. Anthropological approaches of town planning are as follows:

- A city is an abode of different castes, class, religions, and linguistic groups. Therefore, planning of town should be done in such a way which could remove the distance between different caste, religious and linguistic groups and we-feeling could be created.
- In town planning attempt should be made to take care of health and sanitation to all groups and classes.
- Attempt should be made to provide pollution-free air, water and environment.
- In the allotment of houses and land plots, casteism, communalism, regionalism and nepotism must be avoided.
- Every steps should be taken for a prevalence of secular environment in the urban society. Religious centres of all communities should be protected, renovated and beautified.
- Cultural programmes of each community should be encouraged.
- Family welfare programmes must be implemented for good health of mothers and children.
- In jobs and selection procedures, casteism, regionalism, linguism, communalism and nepotism should be discouraged.

- In town planning, attempt should be made to maintain balance between man and nature.
- Town planning should be made keeping a study of post, present scenario and future approach in mind.
- In town planning, the participation of town-dwellers should be invited and their suggestions should be incorporated.
- Town planning should be done keeping ecology in mind.
- Attempt should be made to protect, renovate and beautify the places and monuments which are cultural heritage.
- In town planning special attention should be made on labour class, their residence and every amenities. Because, they play valuable role in development of town.
- Special emphasis should be made for working women and their residences, hostels, hospitals and other amenities.
- Attention should be made on development of sports and gymnasium for youth and parks for children.
- Special attention should be made for displaced group and their rehabilitation.

In this way, anthropological approaches for urban planning emphasises upon human, social and cultural values for the proper development of urban and cosmopolitan society.

Role of Participatory Communication in Town Planning

Now-a-days, special attention is being paid on the role of participatory communication in town planning. According to the concept of participatory communication, the responsibility of urban development is not only limited to administrators and the government, but it also involves the participation of urban society. It is responsibility of members of urban society to explore the problems of their wards and communicate to the administration and government. It is because ward-dwellers know their problems in better way than administration. Therefore, participation of town-dwellers through communication to administrators and government officials can bring more fruitful result in urban planning and achieving the target. Municipality, Municipal Corporation and Ministry of Urban Development are representatives of town-dwellers. People can communicate the problem of their *muhalla* to their representatives and put pressure upon them for inclusion in planning and implementation of development programmes. Thus, participatory communication plays significant role in formulating town planning and implementation of town development programmes.

Advocacy and Plurality of Urban Planning

Now-a-days, a number of organisations have come into existence which are advocating about the urban planning. They are labour organisation, voluntary organisation, commercial organisation, workers organisation, citizen organisation, political organisation, social organisation, cultural organisation and non-governmental organisation. They organise *Dharna,* procession and *Bund, Gherao* and movement for proper urban planning and their implementation. They try to attract the attention of the government towards the interest and problem of urban society. Today Citizen Association, Trader Association, Transporter Association, Rickshaw Association, Auto-rickshaw Association, Bus Owners Association, Footpath Sangh, Vegetable Seller Association, Milk seller Association, Shopkeepers Association and a number of other associations are advocating about urban planning keeping their interest in mind. They are also launching movement for better implementation of town development programmes. Each association has its own problems. Thus, a number of problems emerge for taking care in urban development. The administrator and government consider their some demands and include them in urban planning.

Expansive Area of Urban Planning

The expansive area of urban planning may be as follows:

- Social Area
- Economic Area
- Political Area
- Ecological Area.

Now let us discuss about these expansive areas of town planning one by one in details:

Social Area

Towns, cities and metropolises are centres of different castes, class, religious, linguistic and cultural groups. The problem of each social group are different. They live in separate *muhallas*. For the development of each social group attention should be paid on development of their *muhallas* through road, electricity, water supply, school, colleges, park, community hall and other institutions. Special attention should be given on children, women and aged of each *Muhalla*.

Economic Area

In town planning, emphasis should be made on development of each economic classes. In towns and cities economic classes like labourers, officers, capitalists, traders, businessman, artisans, service doers and workers reside together. Each class—lower, middle and high income group has its own problem which needs to be solved through town planning. Basic amenities like house, water, electricity should be provided to each group. The interests of each group should be taken into account in urban planning. Schools for children and hospitals should be taken care. Transport system and communication system should be developed. Problem of urban youth should be taken into account. The problems of labourers, rickshaw pullers, auto-rickshaw drivers, bus-truck drivers and shopkeepers should be taken into account properly. The problems of displaced groups should be solved at priority level. Traders and businessmen should be given full protection so that they could do their business without any kind of pressure.

Political Area

Under the political areas of urban planning come assembly, residence of all ministers and representatives of each constituencies, residence of Chief Secretary, Court, Justice residence and residences of a number of bureaucrats. They should be provided full protection with all facilities.

Ecological Area

Under ecological area of urban planning come forest area, industrial area, park, tank, river, mountain, *jheel*, bus stand, railway station, drains, street, road, market, malls, cinema halls, tourist places, religious centres, zoo, museum and colonies. They should be protected, renovated and beautified.

Contribution of Anthropologists in Urban Ethnography

Anthropology has made significant contribution in the study of urban ethnography. Anthropologists have studied a number of towns and cities from different angles and have written their ethnography in the form of books, papers and reports about which a detailed description has been given under the chapter "Urban Studies in India". Hence, they are not being repeated here. Readers are requested to read the chapter on Urban Study in India in this book. Urban ethnography has presented before us facts about characteristics of urban society, their origin, structure, function, pathological and other problems. Anthropologists have produced following types of urban ethnography:

- Structure and function of urban family
- Characteristics of urban kinship system
- Religion in urban society
- Administration in urban society
- Urban pathology such as juvenile crime, crimes, beggary vulgarity, truancy and prostitution
- Stability and change in urban family
- Marriage in urban centres
- Administration in urban areas
- Inter-caste relation in urban centre
- Inter-communal relation in towns
- Status of *Bhangi* in urban area
- Status of artisan groups in towns
- Problems of industrial workers
- Industrial sickness
- Concept of neighbourhood in towns
- Consequences of consumerism in cities
- Female focticide in urban area
- Problems of urban women
- Problem of women industrial workers
- Urban health
- Urban sanitation
- Industrial displacement

- Industrial rehabilitation
- Urban culture
- Industrial culture
- Intoxication problems in urban setting
- Urban cultural heritage
- Urban conflict and riots
- Study of slums and *Jhuggi-Jhopari*
- Problem of housing in town
- Land encroachment in urban area
- Problem of *Gundagardi* in towns
- Problem of footpath shopkeepers
- Problem of *tangawala, rickshaw-wala, tempuwala* and *tractor-wala* in towns
- Problem of *Thelawala*
- Problem of hotel and restaurant owners
- Entertainment means in towns
- Problem of water and electric supply
- Problem of transportation and communication
- Occupational mobility in town
- Urban demography
- Crimes in urban area.

Bibliography

Acharya, Hemlata, 1956: 'Urbanising Role of One Lakh City', *Sociological Bulletin*, Vol. V, No. 2.

Ames, Michael M., 1973: 'Family Life in Steel City Jamshedpur', in Milton Singer (ed.) *Entrepreneurship and Modernisation of Occupational Culture in South Asia*, Duke University Monograph No. 12.

Atal, Yogesh, 1961: 'Cult of Bheru in Mewar Village'. *Journal of Social Research*, Vol. IV, No. 12, Ranchi.

Aurora, G.S., 1962: *Tribes, Caste Class Encounter*, Allahabad : Staff Administrative College.

Bailey, F.G., 1958: *Caste and Economic Frontiers*, Oxford University Press, London.

Bailey, F.G., 1959: *Political and Social Change: Orissa*, Oxford University Press, London.

Bailey, F.G. 1960: *Tribes Caste Nation*, Oxford University Press, London.

Banerjee, Debabrata. 1968: *Personality Formation of Unemployed Youth of Calcutta*, Dulal Chand Bhuiya, Sudip Printers, Culcutta.

Bandopadhyay 1963: 'Hira Potters of Assam', *Man in India*, Vol. 43.

Barnabas, A.P., 1969: *Social Life in North Indian Village*, Indian Institute of Public Administration, New Delhi.

Beals, A.R., 1955: 'Interplay Among Factors of Change in Mysore Village' in McKim Marriott (ed.), *Village India*, Chicago.

Beals, A.R., 1955: 'Change in Leadership in a Mysore Village', In: M.N. Srinivas (ed.), *India's Village*, Bombay.

Beals, A.R., 1959: 'Factionalism in a Mysore Village', In: Park and Tinker (ed.), *Leadership and Political Institutions in India*, Oxford.

Beals, A.R., 1962: *Gopalpur: A South Indian Village*, Oxford University Press, Bombay.

Beals, A R., 1971: *Village Life in South India*, Aldine Publishing Company, Chicago.

Beck, E.P. 1972: *Peasant Society in Konku: A Study in Right and Left Hand Caste in South India*, University of British Columbia Press, Vancouver.

Beidelman, T.D., 1959. 'A Comparative Analysis of Jajmani System', *Journal of Augustine*.

Berreman, G.D., 1963: *Hindu of Himalaya,* California University Press, Berkley.

Beteille, Andre, 1960: 'A Note on Pongal Festival'. *Man in India,* Vol. 19.

Beteille, Andre, 1966: *Caste, Class and Power: Changing Pattern of Stratification in Tanjor Village,* Oxford University Press, Bombay.

Beteille, Andre, 1969: *Caste Old and New: Essay in Social Structure and Social Organisation,* Oxford University Press, Bombay.

Bhatt, G.S., 1962: 'Urban Impact and Trend of Inter-Caste Solidarity as a Measure of Status Mobility Among Chamar', *Journal of Social Research,* Vol. V, No. 1, Ranchi.

Biswas, P.C., 1956: *Ex-criminal Tribes of Delhi,* R.P.C., New Delhi.

Bhattacharya, 1896: *Hindu Castes and Sects.* Thacker Spin and Company, Calcutta.

Bhowmick, P.K., 1963: 'Caste and Service in Bengal Village', *Man in India,* Vol. 43.

Blackwood, J.R., 1902: *Calcutta Towns and Suburbs,* Bengal Secretariat Press, Calcutta.

Blunt, E.A.H., 1931: *Caste System in North India,* Oxford University Press, Bombay.

Bopamagame, 1957: *Delhi: A Study of Urban Sociology,* Bombay University, Bombay.

Bose, Ashish, 1962: 'Population Growth, Industrialisation Urbanisation Process in India', *Journal of Social Research,* Vol. 1, Ranchi.

Bose, A.B. and N.S. Jodha, 1965: 'Jajmani System in Desert Village', Vol. 45, No. 2.

Bose, N.K., 1968: *Calcutta: A Social Survey,* Lalvani Publishing House, Bombay.

Bose, A.B. and S.P. Malhotra, 1962: 'Economic Structure of a Village Part in Rajsthan', *Journal of Social Research,* Vol. V, Ranchi.

Bose, A.B. and S.P. Malhotra: 'Socio-economic Difference in Dispersed, Dwelling and Compact Settlement in Arid Region', *Man in India,* Vol. 43, No. 2, Ranchi.

Bose, A.B. and S.P. Malhotra, 1963: 'Anthropo-geographical Settlement Pattern of a Desert Village', *Man in India,* Vol. 44.

Brayne, F.L., 1927: *Village Uplift in India,* London.

Briggs, W.G.,1920: *The Chamars,* Association Press, Calcutta.

Carstairs, G.M., 1957: *The Twice-Born: A Study in High Caste Hindu,* London: Hogarth Press.

Chattopadhyay, G., 1964: 'Carak Festival in West Bengal Village' in L.P. Vidyarthi (ed.), *Aspects of Religion in Asia.*

Chauhan, B.R., 1960: 'An Indian Village: Some Question', *Man in India,* Vol. 4, Ranchi.

Chauhan, B.R., 1970: *Towns is Tribal Setting,* National Publishing House, Delhi.

Chauhan, D.S., 1956: *Trends of Urbanisation in Agra,* Allied Publisher, Bombay.

Cheki, D.A., 1974: *Modernisation and Kinnetwork: Monograph and Theoretical Study in Sociology and Anthropology,* Leiden, E.J. Brill, Netherland.

Cohn, B.S., 1955: 'Changing Status of Depressed Castes in Village India' in McKim Marriott (ed.), *Village India,* Chicago.

Cohn, B.S., 1958: 'Changing Tradition of Low Caste', in Milton Singer (ed), *Traditional India: Structure and Change.*

Crooke, W. 1896: *The Tribes and Castes of North Western Provinces and Oudh,* 4 Volumes, Government Press, Calcutta.

D'Souza, V.S. 1968: *Social Structure of a Planned City.* Orient Longman, Delhi.

Danda, A.K. and D.G. Danda, 1971: *Development and Change in Basudha,* NICD, Hyderabad.

Das, B.M., 1964: 'Kathapara : A Report on Socio-cultural Survey', *Man in India,* Vol. 44.

Desai, I.P., 1964: 'Some Aspects of Family in Malwa', *Journal of Social Research,* Ranchi.

Desai, N.B., 1958: A Report on Administrative Survey on Surat City, Indian Society of Agricultural Economics, Bombay.

Deshmukh, M.B., 1956: 'A Study of Floating Migration', UNESCO Research Centre, Calcutta.

Dhekney, B.C., 1959: *Hubli City: A Study in Urban Economic Life,* Karnataka.

Dhillon, H.S., 1955: *Leadership and Groups in South Indian Village,* Planning Commission, New Delhi.

Dube, S.C., 1952: 'Shamirpet: Social Structure of An Indian Village', *Man in India,* Vol. 32.

Dube, S.C., 1955: 'Ranking of Castes in Telangana Village', in D.N. Majumdar (ed.), *Rural Profile in India,* Lucknow.

Dube, S.C., 1955: *Indian Village,* Routledge and Kegan Paul, London.

Dube, S.C., 1955: 'A Deccan Village' in M.N. Srinivas (ed.), *India's Village,* Bombay.

Dumount, Louis, 1970: *Homo Hierarchicus: An Essay on Caste System.* Chicago University Press, Chicago.

Dutta, A.K., 1962: 'The Neighbourhood Unit Plan and Its Impact on Jamshedpur City', *Journal of Social Research,* Vol. V, No. 1, Ranchi.

Dutta, N.K., 1931: *Origin and Growth of Caste in India,* Oxford University Press, London.

Elwin, Verrier, 1958: *History of Tata Steel,* Bombay

Enthoren, R.E., 1920: *Tribes and Castes of Bombay,* Government Press, Bombay.

Epstein, T. Scarlet, 1959: 'A Sociological Analysis of Witch beliefs in Mysore Village', *Eastern Anthropologist,* Vol. VII, No. 4.

Epstein, T. Scarlet, 1960: 'Economic Development and Peasant Village in South India', *Man in India,* Vol. 40, No. 3.

Epstein, T. Scarlet, 1962: *Economic Development and Social Change in South India,* Manchester Press, London.

Gadgil, A., 1962: *Poona: A Socio-economic Survey,* Gokhale Institute of Politics and Economics, Poona.

Gait, Edward, 1911: *Census of India,* Government Press, New Delhi.

George, K.N., 1956: *Beggar Survey in Madras,* Madras School of Social Work R.P.C.

Ghurye, G.S., 1932: *Caste and Races in India,* Routledge and Kegan Paul, London.

Ghurye, G.S., 1960: *After a Century and a Quarter,* Popular Book Depot, Bombay.

Gore, M.S., 1956: *Beggar Problem of Metropolitan Delhi,* School of Social Work, Delhi.

Gough, E. Kathleen, 1950: "Criteria of Caste Ranking", *Man in India,* Vol. 39, No. 2.

Gough, E. Kathleen, 1955 : 'Social Structure of a Tanjor Village', in M.N. Srinivas (ed.), *India's Village,* Bombay.

Gough, E. Kathleen, 1958: 'Cult of Dead Among Nayar', in Milton Singer (ed.), *Traditional India: Structure and Change.*

Gould, H.A., 1959: 'The Peasant Village: Centripetal and Centrifugal', *Eastern Anthropologist,* Vol. 13, No. 1.

Gould, H.A., 1961: 'A Further Note on Village Exogamy in North India', *South Western Journal of Anthropology,* Vol. 17.

Gould, H.A., 1964: 'Jajmani System of North India: It Structure, Magnitude and Meaning', *Ethnology,* Vol. 3, No. 1.

Grierson, George, 1926: *Bihar Peasant Life,* Government Press, Bihar and Orissa, Patna.

Guha, B.S., 1944: *Racial Elements in Indian Population,* Oxford University Press, Bombay.

Gumperz, J.J., 1958: 'Dialect Difference and Social Stratification in a North Indian Village', *American Anthropologist,* Volume 60.

Harper, E.B., 1959: 'Two System of Exchange in Village India', *American Anthropologist,* Volume 61, No. 5, Chicago.

Harper, E.B., 1959: 'Political Organisation and Leadership in Karnataka Village', in Park and Tinker (ed.), *Leadership and Political Institutions in India.*

Herbert, Paul G., 1971: *Kondru: Structure and Integration in a South Indian Village,* University of Minnesota Press.

Hitchcock, T.J., 1958: 'The Idea of Martial Rajput' in Milton Singer (ed.), *Traditional India: Structure and Change.*

Hitchcock, T.J., 1959: 'The Rajput of Khalapur', Ph.D. Dissertation, Cornell University, USA.

Hitchcock, T.J., 1959: 'Leadership in North Indian Village: Two Case Studies,' in Park and Tinker (ed.), *Leadership and Political Institutions in India*.

Hutton, J.H., 1946: *Caste in India*, Oxford University Press, London.

Ishwaran, K., 1966: *Tradition and Economy in Village India*, Allied Publisher, Bombay.

Ishwaran, K., 1968: *Shivapura: A South Indian Village*, Routledge and Kegan Paul, London.

Ishwaran, K., (ed.), 1970: *Change and Continuity in Indian Village*, Columbia University Press, London.

Iyenger, Keshav, 1957: *Socio-economic Survey of Hyderabad*, Government Press, Hyderabad.

Jack, J.S., 1916: *Economic Life of Bengal District*, Oxford University Press, London.

Jaikar, 1952: *Rural Sweepers in City*, Wesley Press and Publishing House, Mysore.

Kapadia, K.M. and Devendra Pillai (1973): *Industrialisation and Rural Society*, Popular Prakashan, Bombay.

Karve, Iravati, 1953: *Kinship Organisation in India*, Deccan College, Poona.

Kelkar, S.V., 1909: *The History of Caste in India*, Ithaca, Taylor and Carpenter.

Kolenda, P.M., 1958: 'Towards A Model of Hindu Jajmani System', in *Human Organisation*, Vol. 22, No. 1.

Kokade, R.G., 1957: *Socio-economic Survey of Weaving Community of Sholapur*, Gokhale Institute of Politics and Economics, Poona.

Krishna Iyer, L.K.A., 1935: *The Travencore Tribes and Castes*, Vol. I, Government Press, Trivandrum.

Krishna Iyer, L.K.A., 1939: *The Travencore Tribes and Castes*, Vol. II, Government Press, Trivandrum.

Krishna Iyer, L.K.A., 1940: *The Travencore Tribes and Castes*, Vol. III, Government Press, Trivandrum.

Krishna Iyer L.K.A., 1908: *Kochin Tribes and Castes*, Vol. I, Higginbotham and Company, London.

Krishna Iyer, L.K.A., 1912: *Kochin Tribes and Castes*, Vol. II, Higginbotham and Company, London.

Krishna Iyer, L.K.A., 1924: *Mysore Tribes and Castes*, Vol. I, Mysore University Press, Mysore.

Krishna Iyer, L.K.A., 1928: *Mysore Tribes and Castes*, Vol. II, Mysore University Press, Mysore.

Krishna Iyer, L.K.A., 1930: *Mysore Tribes and Castes*, Mysore University Press, Mysore.

Krishna Iyer, L.K.A., 1931: *Mysore Tribes and Castes*, Vol. IV, Mysore University Press, Mysore.

Lakadawala, D.T., 1952: 'Socio-economic Survey of Bombay', *Journal of Social Research*, Vol. 1.

Lakshman Rao, Y.V., 1972: *Communication and Development: A Study of Two Indian Villages*, University of Minnesota Press, Minneapolis.

Lewis, Oscar, 1954: *Group Dynamics in North Indian Village*, Planning Commission, Government of India, New Delhi.

Lewis, Oscar, 1958: *Life in a North Indian Village*, Illinois University, Durban.

Lewis and Burnew, 1965: 'Caste and Jajmani System in North Indian Village', *Scientific Weekly*, Vol. 83.

Leach, E.R., (ed.) 1960: *Aspects of Caste in South India, Ceylone and North West Pakistan*, Cambridge University Press, Cambridge.

Luschiusky, M.S., 1963: 'Problem of Culture Change in Indian Village', *Human Organisation*, Vol. 20.

Maine, H.J.S., 1871: *Village Community in East and West*.

Majumdar, D.N., 1955: 'Rural Profiles', *Eastern Anthropologist*, Ethnographic and Folk Culture Society, Lucknow.

Majumdar, D.N., 1958: *Caste and Communication in Indian Villages*, Asia Publishing House, Bombay.

Majumdar, D.N., 1960: *Chorka Ek Gaon*, Asia Publishing House, Bombay.

Majumdar, D.N., 1960: *Social Contours of an Industrial City*, Asia Publishing House, Bombay.

Malhar, P.M., 1960: 'Changing Religious Practices of an Untouchable Caste', in *Economic Development and Culture Change*.

Malhar, P.M., 1958: 'Changing Caste Ideology in North Indian Village', *Journal of Social Issues*, Vol. 14, No. 4.

Malhotra, P.C., 1964: *Socio-economic Survey of Bhopal and Bairagarh*, Asia Publishing House, Bombay.

Malkani, H.D., 1955: *Socio-economic Survey of Baroda City*, M.S. University of Baroda.

Marriott, McKim, 1955: 'Little Communities in an Indigenous Civilization, *American Anthropologist*, Vol. 57, Chicago.

Marriott, McKim, (ed.) 1955: *Village India*, University of Chicago, Chicago.

Marriott, McKim, 1949: 'International and Attributional Theory of Caste Ranking', *Man in India*, Ranchi.

Marriott, McKim, 1960: *Caste Ranking and Community Structure in Five Regions of India and Pakistan*. Deccan College, Poona.

Mathur, K.S., 1964: *Caste and Rituals in Malwa Village*, Asia Publishing House, Bombay.

Mayer, A.C., 1952: *Land and Society in Malabar*, Asia Publishing House, Bombay.

Mayer, A.C., 1955: 'Change in Malwa Village', *Economic Weekly*, Vol. 7, No. 37.

Mayer, A.C., 1960: *Caste and Kinship in Malwa Village,* Routledge and Kegan Paul, London.

McCormack, W., 1958: 'Sister's Daughter's Marriage in Mysore Village', *Man in India,* Vol. 38, No. 1.

McCormack, W., 1959: 'Factionalism in Mysore Village', in Park and Tinker (ed), *Leadership and Political Institution in India.*

Mishra, Vishwa Mohan, 1972: *Communication and Urbanisation in Urban Slums,* Asia Publishing House, Bombay.

Mishra, B.R., 1959: *Socio-economic Survey of Jamshedpur,* Patna University, Patna.

Mukherjee, P.K. and R.L. Singh, 1961: *Social Problem of Lucknow,* Asia Publishing House, Bombay.

Nayak, T.B., 1957: 'Social Status in Gujrat', *Eastern Anthropologist,* Vol. 10.

Nesfield, J.C., 1885: *Brief View of Caste System of North-Western Province and Oudh,* Government Press, Allahabad.

Nowell, W.H., 1952: 'Gaddi Kinship and Affinal Terms', *Man in India,* Vol. 32, No. 2.

Nowell, W.H., 1955: 'Goshin: A Gaddi Village in Himalayas' in M.N. Srinivas (ed), *India's Village,* Bombay.

O' Mallay, 1932: *Indian Caste System:* Cambridge University Press, London.

O' Mallay, 1934: *India's Social Heritage,* Cambridge University Press, London.

Opler, Morris E., 1956: 'Extension of An Indian Village', *Journal of Asian Study,* Vol. 16.

Oraon, Martin, 1958: 'Tribal People in an Industrial Setting in India', In Milton Singer (ed.), *Traditional India: Structure and Change,* Chicago.

Pandey, Gaya, 2006: *Jatil Samaj Ka Manavshastra,* Concept Publishing Company, New Delhi.

Park, Richard L., 1970: *Urban Bengal,* Michigan University Press, Michigan.

Park, R.L. and Ivene Tinker (ed.), 1959: *Leadership and Political Institutions in India,* Princeton.

Patnayak, N., 1960: 'Out-casting in Oilmen for Drinking Wine', *Man in India,* Vol. 40, No. 1.

Patnayak, N., 1960: 'Barbers and their Clients in an Orissan Village', *Man in India,* Vol. 40, No. 2.

Patnayak, N., 1960: 'Service Relation between Barbers and Villagers in Orissa', *Economic Weekly,* Vol. 12, No. 20.

Prabhu, P.N., 1956: *Study of Social Effect of Urbanisation,* UNESCO Centre, Calcutta.

Prasad, N., 1957: *Myth of Caste System in India,* Patna University, Patna.

Punekar, S.D. and Miss Kamala Rao, 1962: *A Study in Prostitutes of Bombay,* Allied Publisher, Bombay.

Rao, V.K.R.V. and P.B. Desai., 1965: *Greater Delhi: A Study in Urbanisation.* Asia Publishing House, Bombay.

Redfield, Robert, 1930: Tepoztlan, University of Chicago Press, Chicago.
Retzaft, R.H. 1962: *Village Government in India,* Asia Publishing House, Bombay.
Risley, H.H. 1905: *The People of India,* Secretariat Press, Calcutta.
Risley, H.H. 1895: *Tribes and Castes of Bengal,* Government Press, Calcutta.
Robert, Redfield, 1934: *Chankom,* University of Chicago Press, Chicago.
Robert, Redfield, 1941: *Folk Culture of Yucatam,* University of Chicago Press, Chicago.
Robert, Redfield, 1953: *Primitive World and Its Transformation,* University of Chicago Press, Chicago.
Robert, Redfield, 1955: *Little Community Viewpoint for Understanding Human Whole,* Chicago University Press, Chicago.
Robert, Redfield, 1955: *Thinking About Civilization,* Chicago University Press, Chicago.
Robert, Redfield, 1956: *Peasant Society and Culture,* Chicago University Press, Chicago.
Ross, A.D., 1961: *Hindu Family in Urban Setting,* Asia Publishing House, Bombay.
Rosser, K.C., 1952: 'A Hermit Village in Kullu', *Economic Weekly,* Vol. 4.
Rowe, W.L., 1960: 'Social and Economic Mobility in Low Caste in North Indian Community', Ph.D. Dissertation, Cornell University.
Russel, R.V. and Rai Bahadur Hira Lal., 1896: *Tribes and Castes of Central Province of India,* In 4 Vols., Macmillan and Company, London.
Saberwal, Satish (ed.), 1972: *Beyond the Village: Sociological Explorations,* Indian Institute of Advance Study, Shimla.
Sen. S.N., 1961: *The City of Calcutta: A Socio-economic Survey,* Book Land Pvt., Calcutta.
Sen, Lalit Kumar, 1965: 'Family in Four Indian Villages', *Man in India,* Vol. 45, No. 1.
Senart, M.E., 1930: *Caste in India.* Methuen & Company, London.
Sharma, J., 1964: Nuclearisastion of Joint Family in West Bengal', *Man in India,* Vol. 44, No. 3.
Silver, Sen, 1960: *When Caste Barriers Fail.* George Allen and Unwin, Norway.
Sherring, M.A., 1868: *The Sacred City of Hindus Banaras: An Account of Ancient and Modern Times,* London.
Singer, Milton., 1958: 'The Great Tradition in Metropolitan City of Madras', in Traditional India: Structure and Change, *Journal of American Folklore,* Vol. 71, No. 4, Chicago.
Single, R.D., 1956: 'Deity of an Indian Village', *Journal of Asian Study,* Vol. 16, No. 7.
Singh, R.L., 1955: *Banaras—A Study in Urban Geography,* Nand Kishor and Bros.
Singh, T.R., 1961: Hierarchy of Village in Andhra Pradesh', in L.P. Vidyarthi (ed.), *Aspects of Religion in Indian Society,* Ranchi.

Sorley, H.T,. 1933: *City of Bombay, In Census of India, 1931,* Central Government Press, Bombay.

Srinivas, M.N., 1952: *Religion and Society among Coorgs of South India,* Asia Publishing House, Bombay.

Srinivas, M.N., 1962: *Caste in Modern India,* University of California, Berkley.

Srinivas, M.N., 1962: *Caste in Modern India and Other Essays,* Asia Publishing House, Bombay.

Srinivas, M.N., 1966: *Social Change in Modern India,* California University Press, Berkley.

Srinivas, M.N., 1976: *Nation Building in Independent India,* Oxford University Press, Delhi.

Steed, G.P., 1955: 'Personality Formation in Hindu Village in Gujrat', in McKim Marriott (ed.), *Village India,* Chicago.

Vidyarthi, L.P., 1978: *Sacred Complex in Hindu Gaya,* Concept Publishing Co., New Delhi.

Vidyarthi, L.P., 1973: *Researches in Complex Society in India,* New Delhi.

Vidyarthi, L.P., 1977: *Rise of Indian Anthropology,* Vol. II, Concept Publishing Company, New Delhi.

Wiser, W.H., 1936: *Hindu Jajmani System,* Asia Publishing House, Lucknow.

Index

81976 | 57B